To Hunter —

Best wishes for many
successful days chasing
"Dabblers!"

Sincerely
Wade Bourne
4-7-2011

A Ducks Unlimited Guide
to

Hunting

Dabblers

Wade Bourne

A Ducks Unlimited Guide
to

Hunting

Dabblers

Wade Bourne

Ducks Unlimited, Inc.
Memphis, Tennessee

Book Design: Karen Almand
Jacket photograph by Bill Buckley

Published by Ducks Unlimited, Inc.
John A. Tomke, President
Julius Wall, Chairman of the Board
D. A. (Don) Young, Executive Vice President

Distributed by The Globe Pequot Press, P.O. Box 480, Guilford, CT 06437-0480

ISBN: 1-932052-00-3
Published September 2002

Ducks Unlimited, Inc.
Ducks Unlimited conserves, restores and manges wetlands and associated habitats for North
America's waterfowl. These habitats also benefit other wildlife and people. Since its found-
ing in 1937, DU has raised more than $1.3 billion, which has contributed to the conservation
of over 9.4 million acres of prime wildlife habitat in all fifty states, each of the Canadian
provinces, and in key areas of Mexico. In the U.S. alone, DU has helped to conserve over 2
million acres of waterfowl habitat. Some 900 species of wildlife live and flourish on DU projects, including many threatened and endangered species.

Library of Congress Cataloging-in-Publication Data

Bourne, Wade.
    A ducks unlimited guide to hunting dabblers / Wade Bourne.
        p. cm.
    ISBN 1-932052-00-3 (hardcover : alk. paper)
    1. Duck shooting. 2. Anas. I. Title.
SK333.D8 B58 2002
799.2'443--dc21
                                            2002012647

To Hampton B. Bourne,
a fantastic son and an entertaining blind partner

To Haley E. Bourne,
a wonderful daughter with a loving spirit

And to Joe W. Bourne Jr.,
older brother who's still young at heart

Call to Action

The success of Ducks Unlimited hinges upon each member's personal involvement in the conservation of North America's wetlands and waterfowl. You can help Ducks Unlimited meet its conservation goals by volunteering your time, energy, and resources; by participating in our conservation programs; and by encouraging others to do the same. To learn more about how you can make a difference for the ducks, call 1-800-45-DUCKS.

Table of Contents

ACKNOWLEDGMENTS

Many times, duck hunting is a collective effort, and the same is true of writing a duck hunting book. Heartfelt thanks go to everyone who helped directly or indirectly in transforming this book from an idea into printed pages and pictures.

First off, thank you to those hunters around the country who contributed their tips so unselfishly. These men realize that sharing their expertise and helping others enjoy duck hunting is a gift back to their sport. Each contributor is named in the chapter where his special advice is printed. These hunters are benefactors to all who read this book, and they deserve recognition as such.

Special gratitude goes to a short list of others who provided "above and beyond" assistance in my research and production efforts. They include: duck hunting historian and call maker Howard Harlan, world champion duck callers Mike McLemore and Buck Gardner, custom duck call maker Greg Keatts, shotgun experts Ralph Conklin and Jay Conners, decoy maker Dick Gazalski, biologist Dr. Bruce Batt of Ducks Unlimited, writers Chuck Petrie and Matt Young of Ducks Unlimited, and book editor Art DeLaurier Jr. of Ducks Unlimited.

Several reference books were used in research. Two that deserve special mention are *Duck Country*, written by Michael Furtman and published by Ducks Unlimited; and *Flyways: Pioneering Waterfowl Management in North America*, published by the U.S. Fish & Wildlife Service. Both these books are highly recommended for readers interested in furthering their knowledge and appreciation of ducks and the natural history and management thereof.

Duck hunting is best when it's shared with like-minded companions. Through the years I've been blessed with several close friends who have shared my passion for this sport. We have worked together, laughed, succeeded, and failed together, and I love them one and all. They are: Tommy Akin, Ernie Briggs, Don Buck, Wayne Clark, Steve Fugate, Jeff Lannom, Lane Lyle, Phil Sumner, and Don Wright.

My favorite spot in the world for duck hunting and bluegill and bass fishing is Reelfoot Lake in west Tennessee. Mike Hayes operates Blue Bank Resort on Reelfoot's south shore, near Samburg. Thanks to Mike for his warm hospitality and friendship. Thanks also to Blue Bank guides Billy Blakley and Jackie VanCleave for helping me learn my way around this beautiful, bountiful lake.

One special hunting companion is my brother Joe Bourne Jr., who lives in Sugar Land, Texas. My fervent hope is that we can share many more mornings running backwaters and chasing ducks in my boat-blind.

My father, Joe Bourne, instilled in me a love of hunting. My mother, Lucile Bourne, instilled in me a love for life. To Pa and Nana, thanks for all the sacrifices and unwavering support over so many years. I wish other boys could grow up with parents like you. I love and honor you both.

My wife Becky and children Hampton and Haley are the greatest joys in my life. You fill my heart to overflowing; you bless me beyond my ability to express. Thanks for your patience, understanding, and love. I return that love in an immeasurable amount. I hope, long after I'm gone, you'll still be singing, "It's a Beautiful Day."

And ultimately, I acknowledge God as my creator and Christ as my savior. Someday I plan on seeing all my old buddies on that Great Marsh where drought never comes and the ducks always fly.

INTRODUCTION

Pardon me while I gloat.

I've just solved a particularly worrisome problem, and in the process I've once again proved that man is indeed superior to beast. Or at least...sometimes.

I have a four-month-old black Lab puppy named Andy, after Andrew Jackson of late Tennessee fame. (My family has a tradition of naming pets after presidents or first ladies.) During the day, Andy stays in my office, and he continually interrupts my work by tugging or chewing on any target of opportunity. I have to watch him like a hawk. (If my office were more orderly, I wouldn't have this problem, but it's not, and never will be, so I must contend with this pup's energy and the effects of his razor-sharp teeth.)

Andy especially likes to chew on the end of a bentwood rocking chair that sits in front of my fireplace. I've caught him gnawing on it a couple of times and scolded him, but these lessons haven't taken. When I've shifted my attention elsewhere, he's gone back to his conniving work. Now the end of the rocker is burred off like a beaver has attacked it.

How could I solve this problem and convince Andy to quit chewing on the chair without being too heavy-handed? The idea came as I looked around the office: hot sauce! I always keep a bottle of red pepper juice handy—in the house, in my truck, in my boat, and most definitely in my office. This staple is like AA batteries and reading glasses; you can't ever have too many or too much.

So when Andy was distracted, I uncapped the hot sauce bottle and splashed some of its fiery liquid onto the chewed end of the rocker. Then I went back to work and ignored him. The hook was baited.

A few minutes later my pup walked into my workspace licking his lips. And licking them. And licking them! This lesson took. Since then he's never put another tooth mark on the rocker.

So what does this have to do with duck hunting? Here's the association. If I weren't a duck hunter, I wouldn't have Andy, and I wouldn't be privy to the joys of this floppy Lab puppy and all his indiscretions. I wouldn't have the fun of watching him grow and learn new lessons (like, they don't call it *hot* sauce for nothing!). And I wouldn't be the object of his unrestrained affection, of his climbing in my lap and giving me a wet tongue bath. (The *real* discipline lessons will come later.)

Owning a retriever puppy is but one pleasure I take from this sport. There are many others. I take pride in my duck call collection, in spite of the dust the calls gather between hunting seasons. I enjoy the feel and smell of my hunting clothes. They are made for comfort and usefulness instead of show. (There's a lesson on life here, too.) I enjoy shooting a shotgun and smelling a freshly fired hull. I delight in the waterfowl art—prints and decoys—that graces the walls and shelves in my office and home.

But even more, I enjoy the places duck hunting takes me, to America's marshes, bottomlands, rivers, and lakes. Duck hunting is an exercise in adventure and discovery. It is an endeavor of hope in looking for new spots that hold the promise of being the best yet. It is a testing of skills and endurance, a measure of the adage that hard work brings rewards. And duck hunting is a means of getting to know other men and women of like mind. Indeed, duck hunters are a fraternity of the first order. Through the years, my best, most interesting friends are those with whom I've shared blinds and cold mornings. Duck hunters are always characters, and most are people of *good* character.

It is intimidating to write a book of instruction about this sport. There are many duck hunters who have hunted more than I have, who have shot more ducks than I have, and who probably know more than I do. Still, I've hunted ducks passionately for more than 35 years, and I've learned a thing or two along the way. Also, as a career outdoor writer, I've met many expert hunters who were willing to share their knowledge with anybody who would learn from it. I have, and now I pass that knowledge on to you.

As you read, you will discover that "pass it on" is the underlying theme of this book. As I explain in the first chapter, besides the how-tos, "pass it on" also refers to the joys and heritage of duck hunting. It is incumbent upon each veteran hunter to take a youngster or beginner under wing and help him get started. This sport's traditions are too noble and too long-standing to let slip away.

Also, ducks need a strong hunting constituency to ensure their well being. Sport hunters have always been the ones who have stepped forward when these birds were in trouble. Hunters have worked tirelessly for waterfowl, and have provided millions of dollars for conservation work through license sales and donations. Indeed, with all the pressures man has brought on ducks' habitat, it's doubtful that large populations of these birds would exist today if it hadn't been for the support and safeguarding that hunters have provided.

Throughout this book, I refer to the "sport" of duck hunting, "sport" hunting, "sportsmen," etc. Understand that use of the word "sport" in no way represents a connection between duck hunting and score-keeping competitions like football, baseball, golf, and others. Instead, I use the word "sport" in reference to hunting as an activity that is a recreational diversion. "Sport" is also connected to the words "chance" and "fair." Giving ducks or deer or any wild game a "sporting chance" and a "fair chase" is at the core of hunting, an essential element that separates hunters from killers. I've seen some killers in duck hunting, and the sport would have been better off without them.

Duck hunts should be conducted under the rules of fair chase. Game laws should be observed to the letter, to preserve both the birds' welfare and hunters' integrity. Duck hunting shouldn't be a contest to see who can kill the most, or kill the fastest. This isn't to say that a full bag shouldn't be pursued vigorously, but it should be pursued according to the rules and good ethics that separate honorable hunters from the contemptuous.

Throughout this book I use the pronouns "he," "him," and "his." This is done strictly for convenience in writing and by no means indicates any prejudice against women duck hunters. Instead, I believe women hunters may hold the key to the future of duck hunting. In recent years, the number of waterfowl hunters in the U.S. (approximately 1.8 million) has been stagnant—no growth. But if more women enter the ranks, there would be more money spent on licenses and equipment and more support marshaled for the conservation of the duck resource. True, duck hunting has been and is a male-dominated sport, but there's no reason why this cannot and should not change.

Another clarification: I've included no duck recipes in this book. Wild ducks can be delicious, and all the good recipes don't require exotic wines and spices and hours of cooking time. Hunters *should* eat the ducks they shoot, and they will *want* to if they prepare them properly. However, the focus of this book is *hunting* ducks, not *cooking* them. Other authors have covered this latter subject far more adequately than I ever could.

And the same can be said about retriever training, which I've also chosen to leave to the experts. I'm a layman trainer, which means I throw dummies and teach basic discipline in my backyard, but my dogs couldn't compete in field trials. They're simply bodies and noses to fetch my ducks—especially cripples—and they're companions with whom I share much fun and enthusiasm.

There is, however, one area of retriever training in which I excel. If you've got a wooden rocking chair and your pup is gnawing on it and you want him to stop, sprinkle a little hot sauce...
God bless, and good hunting.

Wade Bourne
Clarksville, Tennessee

Chapter One

Overview of Hunting for Dabbling Ducks

Everyone has a few pivotal moments in life that change his history forever. As far as duck hunting goes, my pivotal moment came on a bright December day more than 30 years ago when west Tennessee's Big Sandy River was high and running. This was the morning I went over the edge.

I was in my early 20s, in the Air Force, and home on Christmas leave. Until then I'd been a casual waterfowl hunter. I'd shot ducks several times in preceding years with friends, at their blinds and over their decoys. I'd always enjoyed these outings, but I'd never really embraced this sport. I'd grown up a quail hunter, and my outdoor passion was following the family's two setters through the fields on our corn and tobacco farm.

But that was prior to my milo field enlightenment.

The downpour had started late the previous afternoon and continued past bedtime. A buddy had invited me to join him on a duck hunt the following morning on a water-

Chapter One

fowl management area an hour's drive away. When he picked me up, the rain had slacked, and a cold northwest wind was stirring the night. We could see occasional stars peeking through gaps in the clouds.

We arrived at the area before dawn, but floodwaters had covered the lane to the boat ramp. Instead of launching, we decided to wait for daylight and drive up a road along the edge of the bottom to see if ducks were working.

The milo field was a half mile up this road, bordered by woods on its other three sides. It was some 20 acres in size, and its crop was uncut and standing in long curving rows. Water had risen over the whole field to just a few inches below the reddish-brown heads of grain atop the stalks.

As we watched, a small flight of mallards appeared from over the woods, circled once, and lit on the far end of the field next to the trees. This was all the convincing we needed. My buddy and I pulled on our waders, unloaded his johnboat from his pickup bed, piled in our decoys and shotgun cases, and started paddling between milo rows. Twenty minutes later we were set up in the distant tree line, wind at our side, sun at our back, and decoys bobbing where the ducks had flushed as we approached.

This is when the gates of heaven swung open and the mallards poured out! The first flight was in our spread before we were ready to shoot, 50 or more fanned out and backpedaling to land. The sun reflected brightly off the drakes' iridescent purple green heads and red legs. We fumbled madly with gun cases and shells, but we weren't fast or nimble enough to get loaded before the ducks detected us and flared away.

Overview of Hunting for Dabbling Ducks

We needn't have hurried. In a few minutes another, bigger flight came. This time an over-anxious suzy alerted us by calling down to the decoys. My friend and I froze against our selected trees, fingered our shotgun safeties, and got ready to "lay down the law."

These mallards floated straight in, and we took them just before the lead birds touched the water. Thunder boomed! Pandemonium reigned! Greenheads began dropping, and ducks that hadn't been hit were scrambling for altitude. It was all over in a few seconds. The flight was gone, the shooting sounds had echoed away, and a trail of feathers drifted past us on the last flight they'd ever take.

Soon another flock came, and then another. We took drakes only, and we had our limits in less than a half-hour. Then we called and watched ducks work and reveled in the excitement and beauty of this morning and place.

It was then I realized that this sport thrilled me like no other. Watching those mallards changed me forever, or perhaps it awakened within me some zeal that had been in my hunter's soul but not roused until that morning. It was a feeling the likes of which I'd never experienced. I knew on the ride home that ducks and wet places and cold mornings would be essential parts of my life from that day forward. And so they have been.

I'm certain that legions of other duck hunters throughout North America have had similar awakenings. I say *certain* because the evidence speaks for itself. Duck hunters are a dedicated band of brothers and sisters. They go to extraordinary lengths to enjoy their sport. They expend enormous effort, endure harsh conditions, pay princely sums of money, and scheme year-round about how to make the next season better than the last. Duck hunters revel in each other's company. They speak a common language. They share similar histories and hopes. Non-hunters don't understand this keenness and camaraderie. They can't fathom why otherwise sane people rise from bed at unholy hours, head off into the dark and cold, leave their families, forsake their jobs, and sometimes risk their lives, just for the chance to bag a few birds like those they feed at the local park.

They just don't know. When a duck hunter gets it all right, the satisfaction is sublime. When he picks the precise spot, fashions a good blind, sets his decoys to look like live ducks on the water, calls convincingly, and makes a clean kill, and when his retriever fetches his game efficiently and obediently, he has reached a high pinnacle of achievement. Through this feat comes the gratification of a job done well and the fulfillment of some primitive instinct to bring meat back to the campfire (kitchen).

This book has two main purposes. The first purpose is to celebrate this sport and to honor its participants and the birds they pursue. Duck hunting is truly an endeavor of the heart. The connection between hunter, setting, and game stirs deep emotions of hope, joy, and respect.

This book's second purpose is to help others be more successful at duck hunting. Greater enjoyment comes through successes afield. True, failures are measuring rods for successes, and we need failures to make successes sweeter. But honing his skills should be a goal of every hunter who pursues waterfowl or other game, and one of the best ways to do this is to borrow from the knowledge of veterans who are willing to share what they know.

I am willing to share, and so are the many others who have contributed unselfishly to this book. It's a privilege to help other hunters enjoy this sport, and personally, I believe it's also an obligation. This is because, when we were gathering up our decoys and preparing to paddle back out of the milo field so many years ago, when I was sky-high with enthusiasm for the events of that morning and for the prospects of future, similar mornings, I heard a whisper that came from the air, or the water, or maybe from within my soul. Its message: "Pass it on."

Dabbling Ducks: An Overview

To be more specific, I am a *dabbling* duck hunter, as are the majority of duck hunters in North America. I may take an occasional scaup, canvasback, ringneck, or other diving duck over my dabbler decoys. However, the species I target are members of the tribe Anatini: mallards, pintails, black ducks, gadwall, American wigeon, teal (blue-winged, green-winged, cinnamon), wood ducks, northern shovelers, and mottled ducks. (For detailed reviews of these species, refer to *Duck Country*, written by Michael Furtman and published by Ducks Unlimited. This excellent book provides in-depth information about these birds and the dynamic factors that form their natural history.)

Dabbling ducks are also called "puddle ducks." They feed mostly in shallow water—a foot or less in depth. They are omnivorous, consuming both animal and vegetable matter.

Their diet consists mostly of aquatic plants, wild seeds, and cultivated grains. They also eat some invertebrates and small vertebrates, especially to increase their protein intake just before the mating and nesting season.

The norm is for dabbling ducks to feed mostly in early morning and late afternoon and to spend midday periods loafing and preening on land at water's edge.

"Dabblers" derive their name from their method of surface

feeding. They tip up—head underwater and tail pointing skyward. These ducks are capable of diving, especially when pursued, but most of their feeding is done while they are on or barely beneath the water. Also, some dabbling ducks routinely feed on dry land. Their legs are situated toward the center of their body, which balances their weight and makes them adept at walking in fields, on sandbars, etc.

Dabblers dabble, tipping up to feed on aquatic vegetation, grain, and invertibrates just below the water's surface.

Dabbling ducks possess another anatomical

advantage: long wings that allow them to spring directly into the air from water or land—no long running starts like diving ducks. Startle them, and they can be airborne in an instant.

Most dabbling duck species (except black ducks and mottled ducks) are dimorphic in plumage. That is, the mating plumage of the drakes is different—and typically more colorful—than the plumage of the hens. However, during the summer molt, drakes grow drab plumage similar to that of hens so they can hide from predators during the 2- to 3-month period when they cannot fly. When flight feathers come back in, this plain "eclipse" plumage is replaced by the brighter mating coloration, usually by the time the fall migration is starting.

Dabblers nest throughout a broad range of North America, from Alaska to Mexico, and from east coast to west. However, the great majority of these birds are produced in the Prairie Pothole Region of the north-central U.S. and prairie Canada (Manitoba, Saskatchewan, and Alberta). In this area, glaciers of the last ice age scoured the land and left thousands of shallow depressions that seasonally fill with rainwater and melted snow. Dabbling ducks use these small, temporary wetlands to raise their broods.

Most hens actually nest in adjacent dry ground cover, then quickly move their newly hatched ducklings to water, where they are safer from predators. Thus numbers of these birds fluctuate up and down depending on the abundance of water and the lushness of nearby upland cover. When water and cover are plentiful, duck numbers can increase dramatically. When water and cover are scarce, these numbers can plummet at an equally fast rate. The ongoing cycles of abundant moisture and drought are major factors in the long-term fluctuations in continental populations of these birds.

By early fall, adult ducks and their young-of-the-year begin collecting in large flocks on staging areas, the first step of their migration to southern wintering areas. The timing of this migration depends on species and weather patterns. Most blue-winged teal will leave the prairie at the onset of fall, usually in late August or September. Other early migrants (but not this early) include pintails and gadwall. In contrast, mallards are hardy birds that will stay on northern prairies until potholes freeze over and snows pile up so deep they can no longer find food.

The pace of the fall migration can be directly affected by the severity (or lack thereof) of fall weather. A strong cold front can move millions of ducks southward overnight (called a "grand passage"). On the other hand, a mild fall can lead to a "trickle down" migration where ducks stay up north longer and migrate southward in less spectacular numbers and over a longer period of time.

In this sense, one group of hunters' gain is another group's loss. When winter comes early to northern prairies and hurries ducks southward, hunting is usually fast and furious in northern states,

A mixed bag of dabblers—mallards, gadwall, and wigeon.

Overview of Hunting for Dabbling Ducks

These hunters enjoy the bounty of dabblers wintering in Mississippi flooded timber.

before the birds have passed through and the water is frozen. In this situation, hunters farther down the flyways benefit from the arrival of "new ducks" in their areas. Conversely, when fall is mild and the migration is delayed, northern hunters have a better season because the ducks stick around longer, while hunters in mid-latitude and southern states experience poor hunting due to a scarcity of new arrivals from up north.

On their wintering grounds, ducks tend to concentrate on traditional areas where habitat is good, food is available, and some measure of protection is afforded on refuges and private holdings where hunting pressure is controlled. Each of the four major flyways, identified through flight banding studies (see next section) has several such areas. Traditional wintering grounds in the Atlantic Flyway include Chesapeake Bay, North Carolina's coastal region, South Carolina's ACE Basin, and eastern Florida's upper St. Johns River complex. In the

Chapter One

Mississippi Flyway, eastern Arkansas' bottoms and rice country, Tennessee's Reelfoot Lake, Mississippi's Delta, and Louisiana's coastal marshlands hold the majority of wintering birds.

In the Central Flyway, primary wintering areas include the Texas Panhandle's playa lakes; the same state's rice prairie (west of Houston), Trinity River delta (east of Houston), and Gulf Coast; New Mexico's Bosque del Apache refuge; and the Yucatan peninsula in northeastern Mexico. And in the Pacific Flyway, primary wintering areas include the South Columbia Basin in southeastern Washington, the Willamette Valley in Oregon, the Central Valley in California, and coastal lagoons in the states of Sonora and Sinaloa in western Mexico.

On these wintering grounds, duck concentrations can shift quickly and dramatically in response to changes in water and food conditions. For instance, if heavy rains flood hardwood forests along eastern Arkansas' White and Cache rivers, mallards will abandon this area's rice fields and move en masse to the newly inundated green timber. Researchers have radio-tracked ducks' movements enough to learn that they are highly mobile and have some method for communicating the urgency for changing locations. This is why, in a given region, ducks can literally be here today and gone tomorrow. Virtually an entire concentration can move somewhere else overnight.

Dabbling ducks aren't just eating and biding time on their wintering grounds. Their intricate ritual of courtship and pair bonding begins here. Older, bigger drakes tend to be more successful at attracting mates. Once paired, a drake and hen will stay together during the spring migration back north, where their ages-old cycle of breeding and nesting will start over.

Dabbling ducks are extremely hardy birds. Nature has equipped them with instincts and resilience to face a broad range of adversities. They can endure droughts, storms, and other weather extremes. They can withstand the rigors of twice-a-year migrations over thousands of miles. They have an amazing reproductive tenacity. They can find food and evade predators and carry out other life essentials with incredible efficiency.

Perhaps the only real threat to their survival is man, and more specifically, man-caused destruction of the habitat these birds need to live. If North America's potholes, marshes, swamps, oxbows, and alluvial bottoms are preserved, large-scale duck populations will survive—indeed, thrive—over the long term. But if these wetlands continue to be lost, wildfowl's future will disappear with them, replaced by a sad decline of

© Bill Buckley

one of nature's greatest wildlife spectacles. The Grand Passage will be no more, and mankind will bear the responsibility.

The choice to save or destroy is ours.

Short History of Duck Hunting in North America

These 2,000-year-old canvasback decoys were unearthed in Nevada in 1924. ©M. R. Harrington, 1924 C/O The National Museum of the American Indian, Smithsonian Institution.

Natural historians know that ducks have long been the targets of hunters in North America. In 1924, anthropologists digging an American Indian site in Nevada unearthed a basket containing 11 canvasback decoys that had been carefully crafted from reeds and natural skins, then wrapped and stored some 2,000 years ago (as determined by carbon-dating). This is the first hard evidence of waterfowl hunting on this continent, though surely ducks have been targeted by man for as long as the two have co-existed here. American Indians are known to have trapped and netted waterfowl and even to have caught them by hand by swimming underneath a resting flock and snatching birds underwater to drown them.

Duck hunting changed dramatically when white settlers arrived on the East Coast. Early colonists described huge concentrations of wildfowl and their use of these birds as a ready food source. These immigrants brought their fowling pieces with them from England, France, Holland, and other countries. During the 1700s and early 1800s, many ducks were killed over ponds and marshes around Chesapeake Bay, Delaware Bay, Lake Mattamuskeet and the Outer Banks in North Carolina, and other areas of waterfowl abundance.

As settlers pushed across the Appalachian Mountains, they discovered the greatest concentration of waterfowl in North America in a corridor 200 miles either side of the Mississippi River, from Canada to the Gulf of Mexico. The Father of Waters and its tributaries encompassed a sprawling network of oxbows, bottomlands, and marshes that became the epicenter of duck hunting in the years that followed. The Illinois River bottoms, Reelfoot Lake and the Obion and Forked Deer river bottoms in Tennessee, Big Lake and the White and Cache river bottoms in Arkansas, and Catahoula Lake and the coastal marsh in Louisiana were a few of many places where waterfowl collected in incredible numbers. During his wanderings in the early 1800s, painter-hunter John James Audubon reported concentrations of ducks, geese, and swans that literally blackened the sky along the lower Mississippi.

This seemingly limitless number of birds spawned a lively commercial trade in wildfowl. Market hunting reached its zenith in the mid- to late 1800s, supplying waterfowl by the barrel for markets in New York, Philadelphia, Chicago, St. Louis,

Memphis, New Orleans, and other large cities. Market hunters became highly efficient at providing canvasbacks, mallards, and other tasty species to eager consumers. During this period, many hotel dining rooms offered wild duck dinners for what was then the princely sum of $2 to $3.

Sport hunting of waterfowl began to evolve in this same era. Duck clubs sprang up at prime duck and goose stopovers along the East Coast, the Great Lakes, and the Mississippi Valley. Members of these clubs typically were well-to-do people who had money to spend on the various trappings of this sport. Carvers supplied their demand for decoys from backyard workshops, especially in eastern states where diving ducks were the main targets, and decoying them was the principal hunting strategy. Other centers of decoy carving developed in Illinois and Louisiana, and eventually commercial decoy factories were built to meet the growing market from hunters who found that using wooden or canvas decoys was more practical than keeping live decoys year-round.

Duck calls and calling trace their roots to the Mississippi Valley. Mallards were the predominant duck in this region, and hunters learned that imitating their calls helped in coaxing (with decoys) these birds to land or—in the case of timber hunters—to come to the sounds of feeding ducks and splashing water. Duck calling was honed to a fine art in this area, which today remains the country's center for call making and calling contests.

As settlers continued pushing westward, other areas in other flyways became hubs of duck hunting: the pothole region of the Dakotas, Nebraska's Sandhills and Platte River complex,

Kansas's Cheyenne Bottoms, northwest Texas's playa lakes, Utah's Great Salt Lake marsh, California's Central Valley, Oregon's Willamette Valley, and others. Wherever ducks were available, hunters were there to pursue them.

However, by the late 1800s duck numbers began to decline due to unrestricted shooting by both market and sport hunters, and the wholesale draining and clearing of wetlands. What once seemed an endless supply of birds dwindled to an alarming degree. Early conservationists began fearing a repeat of the passenger pigeon debacle. New rules had to be put in place to control the slaughter, and wetlands loss had to be controlled to ensure that duck and goose populations would be perpetuated for the benefit and pleasure of future generations.

Thus the modern era of waterfowl conservation took root. The Migratory Bird Act of 1913 was the first effort to bring waterfowl management under federal control and to impose a uniform system of harvest regulations throughout the states. This act also banned market hunting, shotguns larger than 10-gauge, and hunting during spring, when ducks were migrating back to their northern nesting grounds. After five years of wrangling and legal challenges by states' rights advocates, this act was signed into law in 1918. At that time the U.S. Bureau of Biological Survey (USBS, the forerunner to the U.S. Fish & Wildlife Service) assumed responsibility for managing waterfowl and enforcing related game laws.

It was also during this period that one simple management tool transformed the way waterfowl were monitored and hunting seasons were regulated: the leg band. Banding traces its roots back to John James Audubon and his wrapping of silver wire around the legs of a brood of eastern phoebes near his home in Mill Grove, Pennsylvania, in 1803. The following year two of these birds returned, completing the first banding study. Latter-day biologists seized on Audubon's idea and expanded it exponentially.

Leg banding on a large scale was undertaken in the early 1900s. By 1929 more than 400,000 waterfowl had been banded, and more than 19,000 leg bands had been recovered. Migration patterns could be plotted from this leg band data.

Leg bands continue to play a major role in furthering our understanding of waterfowl movements.

Biologists learned that ducks and geese followed four broad flyways when traveling between nesting and wintering areas. They named these corridors the Atlantic, Mississippi, Central, and Pacific flyways and began tracking bird numbers according to these geographical demarcations. Also, data from leg bands provided impetus for expanding a fledgling system of national wildlife refuges. During the 1920s, several new refuges were established at vital waterfowl sites, and significant funds were secured for adding to and maintaining this chain of waterfowl sanctuaries.

Today biologists know that waterfowl's migration patterns are much more complex than this division into four major flyways suggests. Still, this management concept remains in use and has proved its worth in splitting the continent's waterfowl population into manageable units. This is how the system of different season and harvest frameworks in the four flyways came into being.

Modern biologists also understand that waterfowl production is directly linked to the quality of habitat in nesting areas, and for dabbling ducks especially, quality of habitat is determined by the abundance—or scarcity—of water. Historically, northern nesting areas have undergone several-year cycles of plentiful moisture and booming duck numbers, followed by years of drought and low duck numbers.

The worst drought on record lasted from 1915 to 1934. During these years thousands of potholes dried up and were plowed through by prairie farmers. Duck numbers dwindled to a critically low point. Drastic action had to be taken quickly to stem this loss of birds and preserve a core population from which waterfowl numbers could rebuild when conditions turned more favorable.

This near-catastrophe turned out to be a blessing in disguise. Government and private conservationists, supported by public-spirited citizens, tackled the waterfowl issue with great urgency. New laws were enacted, including the Migratory Bird Hunting Stamp Act (1934), which required all hunters sixteen years of age or older to purchase an annual federal duck stamp. (This act was lobbied for tirelessly by J. N. "Ding" Darling, a Pulitzer-winning cartoonist who later became director of the U.S. Biological Survey.) Implementation of this act immediately raised millions of dollars for the purchase and development of waterfowl habitat.

Shooting ducks over bait was banned in 1935. Hunting over live decoys was abolished in 1937. In this same year, the Pittman-Robertson Act levied an 11 percent excise tax on the purchase of certain sporting goods to raise funds for state wildlife agencies. Many of these Pittman-Robertson tax dollars have been funneled into waterfowl management projects.

Also, Ducks Unlimited was founded in 1937 to raise money from sportsmen for the preservation of wetland habitat on the Canadian prairie. During its history, DU has raised more than $1.7 billion for waterfowl management and conserved some 10.3 million acres of prime habitat in Canada, Mexico, and the U.S.

Since it was founded in 1937, Ducks Unlimited has contributed to the conservation of more than 10.3 million acres of wildlife habitat in North America.

During the late 1930s a new, more accurate system for surveying waterfowl populations was devised. This system involved using human census takers in airplanes, cars, and boats to cover the same survey routes year after year. By comparing pond count and brood data from one nesting season to the next, biologists could interpret trends in waterfowl populations over the long term.

During this same era, Aldo Leopold led the way in professionalizing the science of wildlife management, and the Division of Migratory Waterfowl was created within the U.S. Biological Survey. Thus progress toward saving the ducks was made on several fronts. Many pegs were now in place for providing a safety net for this great resource. Finally, when rains returned to the prairie, the ducks did likewise.

From the early 1940s until now, duck populations have risen and fallen according to water conditions on the nesting grounds. Wetlands have continued disappearing to the dragline and plow in both nesting and wintering areas. Waterfowl

The health of waterfowl populations depends largely on water conditions on nesting grounds such as these in the north-central U.S. and prairie Canada.

census procedures have been refined even more. Season lengths and bag limits have been adjusted and readjusted according to annual survey findings.

The system of modern management is far from perfect, but it continues to improve. New technologies (computer models, satellite imagery, etc.) provide biologists with better data to predict population trends and to solve problems. While still dependent on nature to provide moisture for the nesting grounds, conservationists are now better equipped with knowledge, funds, manpower, and sweeping conservation programs

Chapter One

(CRP, Swampbuster) to see ducks through dry years and to help maximize their production when water is plentiful.

The history of duck hunting in North America is one of boom to bust...then recovery. Biologists and sportsmen have learned that the duck resource is fragile and can suffer precipitous drops, but when good habitat returns, population recovery can be dramatic and fast. It is the role of government agencies, conservation groups like Ducks Unlimited, and private citizens to work together to shepherd waterfowl populations through difficult times, and to enjoy and share their abundance when numbers are high.

Duck Hunting Today

If duck hunting were a buffet, modern hunters would have difficulty deciding on a main course. There are so many appealing options. Hunters can pursue dabbling ducks in marshes both north and south. They can hunt them on open lakes or in bottomland timber, on big rivers or small streams, in flooded or dry fields, in swamps, on beaver ponds and stock ponds, and in other settings where these birds collect and hunting is allowed. Many of these are naturally formed places that have drawn ducks for eons. Others are man-made, some to serve expressly as hunting areas and refuges. Many are on public property, many more on private.

Each hunter must find his own spots and choose his hunting methods. These decisions will be made based on availability, capability, and federal and state game laws. But there is a lot of room under these umbrellas. Hunters who wish to pursue ducks have broad opportunities for doing so.

Overview of Hunting for Dabbling Ducks

This may not seem so at first, particularly on heavily hunted public areas. Many waterfowl areas around the U.S. draw large crowds, and competition for good spots is stiff. Some areas are regulated by a permit lottery system, and you have to apply for permits long before the season starts.

However, I know firsthand that good hunting on public areas is available to hunters who learn the rules and who are willing to work hard to find it. I hunt extensively on public areas. Some of my favorite spots are on management units where hunter numbers are closely restricted in certain areas, but where unlimited freelance hunting is available on other areas. Frequently, these freelance areas are overlooked by hunters who don't have the know-how or the equipment to take advantage of them. I have both, and I enjoy great public hunting that most hunters don't even know exists.

I also hunt on large rivers and reservoirs that are wide open to the public. I know that hunters who make a concerted effort can find great hunting on these waters, perhaps not every day, but certainly when changing conditions cause ducks to shift to them from other areas.

"Concerted effort" is the key phrase for modern duck hunters. Unless you buy a membership in a private duck club or a lease to hunt private land (for which you'll pay a prince's ransom), securing quality duck hunting takes work. It requires hours of investigation, the maintaining of good contacts, repeated scouting trips, and much trial and error to turn up leads and check them out. Some "discoveries" won't pan out, but every now and then you'll find a gem that will provide good hunting like my spots have for me. (Chapter 6 in this book goes into great detail about scouting and collecting information on potential hunting spots.)

The point is, good public duck hunting spots are available to

© Bill Buckley

hunters who are serious about finding them. This effort must be deliberate, focused, and long running, but the places are out there waiting for the hunter with the determination to ferret them out.

Getting to where the ducks are is seldom a walk in the park.

Another issue facing modern duck hunters is modern technology and the development of gadgets that make bagging ducks easier. In decoys especially, there is a whole range of new electrically-powered motion devices like wing-spinners and shaker decoys that have a strong attraction to ducks. Some hunters believe using these devices makes duck hunting too easy, that such devices replace skill with "widgetry" and should thus be banned.

However, in most states these devices are allowed by law (check regulations in your state), and many hunters use them. My philosophy is that if such devices are legal, they are OK from an ethical standpoint. If a hunter personally opts not to use them, that's his choice. If a governing agency determines at some point that use of these devices is threatening or harming the resource, then they will outlaw them.

One other consideration for modern duck hunters is that of hunter ethics and behavior in the field. In some hunters, increased competition causes a "get mine at any cost" attitude, which leads to ill-mannered conduct and even to the violation of game laws. There is no room for compromise in this area. Every hunter must hunt responsibly, legally, and with full considera-

tion for the rights of other hunters. This is the proper thing to do, and it is the right attitude to pass along to young and beginning hunters.

Since my milo field hunt more than three decades ago, I've seen many ducks drop into decoy spreads around the country. (I've also seen many more fly away that should have dropped.) I've watched many beautiful sunrises over marsh, swamp, lake, and field. I've shared charcoal buckets and swapped tales with some of the country's best guides and hunters. I've developed new hunting spots—or tried to—and I've found other places where hunting is consistently good when the ducks are in.

Duck hunting's future. The author's son, Hampton Bourne, with a brace of mallards (above), and a young hunter with a prize pintail (below).

Chapter One

If there has been one constant thread in all these people and places and experiences, it's that ducks are fairly predictable most of the time, but certainly not all the time. When you think you've got them figured out, they'll do something totally unpredictable, and you'll get another helping of humble pie that all duck hunters must eat from time to time. However, it's this uncertainty in the sport and the ongoing quest for improvement that makes it fun.

The following chapters are devoted to calling, rigging and setting decoys, building blinds, and handling other chores that go into successful duck hunting. But as you learn, keep in mind that *how* is more important than *how many*. When you hunt, hunt with respect—for your quarry, for your fellow hunters, and ultimately for yourself. Do your best to bag your birds, but better yet, do your best to *be* your best. And pass it on.

Chapter Two

Hunting Tactics

The small hole of open water was every duck hunter's dream.

It was several hundred yards back in a swamp, isolated from other holes and blinds where ducks got blistered when they tried to land. But this opening was a haven where mallards, gadwall, black ducks, and other species could drop in unmolested, then swim out into the timber and sawgrass to feed or rest. Or at least it was a haven until I found it. Then it became my own personal honey hole.

I'd seen ducks working this area before, and I decided to go prospecting. The going was difficult, weaving my boat through trees and grass, hanging up on logs and shallow spots, push-poling and wading and pulling to get through tight places. After 30 minutes of such work, I felt like I'd been through a football workout.

But what I discovered was worth the effort! The thick cover finally parted to reveal a small, hidden pond. It stretched approximately 25 yards across, and it was bordered by cypress trees, sawgrass, and a beaver hut on the northeast corner. Its "chemistry" was perfect for ducks—the right size, cover, isolation. I knew this was where I'd been seeing birds go in, and I was excited about the prospects of hunting it.

But I wasn't the first hunter to have been here. Remnants of an old blind were hanging from two cypress trees at the south end of the pond. Only a couple of weathered boards were left, but they were enough to show that years or even decades ago somebody else had fought his way in like I had and built a hiding spot to take his own toll of ducks. How I'd like to talk to him!

I wouldn't build a blind here, as he'd done. Instead, I'd bring my blind with me, attached to my boat. My decoys would also go in and out. When I left after a hunt, there would be no sign of my having been there except perhaps some bent-over grass.

What satisfactions—and disappointments—would I encounter here in seasons ahead? Where would I situate my boat blind, and how should I set my decoys to be most convincing to passing birds? How good *would* this place be?

Such anticipations are among the great pleasures in duck hunting—trying new spots, making new plans, daydreaming about them between hunts and seasons. Duck hunters are eternal optimists. Despite how successful the last season was, next year's can be better, and there are always fresh schemes for making it so.

For instance, freelance hunters like me continually search for that latest, best spot. And hunters who hunt the same place year after year continuously change their blinds, decoy spreads, and methods for managing lure crops and water levels in an effort to find a better duck hunting "recipe."

One of the most enjoyable aspects of hunting dabbling ducks is this sport's diversity. These birds are found in marshes, swamps, open lakes, rivers, flooded timber, flooded fields, dry fields, etc. Each of these settings offers unique challenges and opportunities, and each requires its own different methods to hunt effectively. Consistent duck hunting success stems from knowing how to match tactics to locations and conditions with which you're presented. Hunters who are can adapt the best typically bag more birds.

Following are time-proven methods for hunting in various types of terrain, and also how to change strategies when new conditions dictate the prudence of doing so.

Freelancing Versus Fixed-Blind Hunting

There are two basic options for hunting dabbling ducks: freelancing and fixed-blind hunting.

The names offer accurate descriptions of the tactics. The freelance hunter moves from spot to spot according to changing conditions and hunting opportunities. He follows the ducks, typically by boat, ATV, or on foot. He sets out small- to medium-sized portable decoy spreads. He chooses his gear for convenience in moving about. His mindset is "run and gun," and he scouts continually during hunting season to decide where to try each new day.

On the other hand, the fixed-blind hunter is a homesteader. He hunts from a permanent blind that is affixed to one site or

© Bill Buckley

ATVs have become an important tool for getting hunters into hard-to-reach areas.

small area that ducks regularly frequent. Instead of moving to the ducks, the fixed-blind hunter waits for the ducks to come to him. He occupies his blind, spends his allotted hunting time, and hopes the birds show up.

Each of these hunting methods has its advantages and drawbacks. Because of his mobility, the freelancer is more versatile. If fresh rains spawn a flood, he can run backwaters and look for ducks in newly inundated fields or green timber. Or if a hard freeze locks up shallow marshes and flooded fields, the freelancer can shift to big lakes or rivers where water is still open and ducks are now concentrated. The major premise of freelancing is being able to go where the ducks go *when* they go there.

The main drawbacks of freelancing are the gear, effort, and time commitment required for this style of hunting. Freelancing is no casual undertaking. Freelance hunters usually need a boat and motor, portable blind, and other specialized gear. Frequently a four-wheel-drive vehicle and/or an ATV are needed to get into hard-to-reach duck spots. Freelancers must also maintain a list of contacts to help them keep up with duck movements and the best hunting opportunities. Without good intelligence, freelance hunting is a hit-or-miss proposition at best.

The main advantages of fixed-blind hunting are convenience and comfort in a proven spot. Most of the work is done before the season starts. Just show up, toss out the decoys (if they're not already out), and wait for the ducks to arrive. Indeed, waiting is easier in a comfortable blind than when standing in water or huddled in bushes on a muddy bank. And generally, the longer you wait, the greater the chance the ducks will eventually fly. The main premise of fixed-blind hunting is being in a spot that ducks use on a daily basis and sticking around until they come.

The obvious drawback to fixed-blind hunting is that sometimes the ducks *don't* show up. If they've shifted somewhere else, the fixed-blind hunter is doomed to stare at empty skies.

Perhaps the best approach to hunting dabbling ducks is to practice both methods. When ducks are working predictable areas and patterns, fixed-blind hunting can be very productive. But when conditions change and a special opportunity arises, a hunter should have the capability to take advantage of it through freelancing.

How much farther? When you're freelancing, a half-mile hike can seem like a 100-mile journey.

Chapter Two

A partner and I flood a field and maintain a pit blind in a river bottom a few miles from my home. Our spot is situated beneath a flyway between a national wildlife refuge and a state public hunting area. Ducks gang up on the refuge, and each day some usually fly upriver to the hunting area, which has several flooded cornfields. To get to this banquet, they fly over our pond spread of some 400 duck and Canada goose decoys. With this spread and our loud, persuasive style of calling we can usually draw a few into shooting range.

Sometimes, though, action gets slow in the bottoms, or I hear about better hunting elsewhere. I keep a boat rigged with a portable blind and loaded with decoys for freelancing. I can hook up the boat trailer and be gone in short order. Over the years, many of my best hunts have come on such spur-of-the-moment opportunities.

Again, overall success in duck hunting comes from being versatile and knowing how to adapt to different settings and situations. Following is a list of common duck hunting scenarios and strategies for taking birds in each case.

Hunting in Swamps and Marshes

Swamps and marshes exist virtually everywhere ducks are found. These natural wetlands are diverse in their make-up, character, and size. From the potholes of the northern prairie to the Gulf coastal marsh, from East Coast swamplands to tule flats in California, swamps and marshes are magnets to dabbling ducks and offer a diverse range of hunting challenges.

But despite their location and diversity, the same general hunting strategy applies: find where ducks are working, and

move to them. Figure out which potholes or areas of a swamp or marsh are most attractive to the birds, then go there. In duck hunting, there's no substitute for being in the right spot.

Swamps and marshes can be hunted by both freelancers and fixed-blind hunters. Freelancers obviously can move about daily and set up where they wish. Fixed-blind hunters build their blinds in holes or pockets that ducks use on a regular basis. Many such spots are under natural flight lanes that ducks follow

Hunting in marsh country: A hunter takes advantage of natural cover as he takes aim at overhead ducks (above), while another hunter tosses decoys into a prairie pothole (below).

when trading between resting and/or feeding areas.

For freelance hunters, having a way to penetrate swamps and marshes is crucial to success. Big boats and motors can be more of a burden than a help. Smaller, maneuverable boats that draw less water are more functional. Johnboats, canoes, pirogues, Poke Boats, and similar craft are perfect for getting into thick spots that bigger boats can't reach. Sometimes paddling or push-poling is the only way to reach a honey hole.

After more than four decades of duck hunting, I've settled on the Go-Devil boat and motor as the ideal freelance rig for swamps and marshes. Quite simply, this combination metal boat and long-shaft direct-drive motor will take a hunter places he couldn't dream of going in a conventional johnboat and outboard. The Go-Devil boat has a semi-V bow and a flat bottom for riding through and over brush, vegetation, stumps, and logs. The motor is a workhorse that will power the boat through thick cover and shallow water. (My boat will run in 5 inches of water.)

My 16-foot Go-Devil boat is perfect for carrying two hunters, a retriever, two large bags of decoys, and other required gear. It's

© Wade Bourne

rigged with an Avery Quick-Set portable blind. I can follow ducks through dense swamps with this rig, leaving other hunters behind. When I decide to set up, I can toss out my decoys, hide the boat, and

The Go-Devil boat and motor make an ideal rig for plowing through thick cover and shallow water.

raise the blind, all in less than 10 minutes. Then, if the spot doesn't pan out, I can quickly take the blind down, pick the decoys up, and move somewhere else.

Hunters who aren't similarly equipped can still have great shooting in swamps and marshes by boating or wading in, then hiding in natural cover. Nothing is more effective than hunkering in cattails or in the folds of a cypress or tupelo tree. However, this style of hunting can be uncomfortable. Some type of marsh seat or even a plastic bucket can be a back saver (for boat-in hunters only, not waders).

Modern camouflage clothing is super for helping hunters disappear into terrain. Wear clothes that will blend in with natural cover. Also, when picking a hunting site, if the wind allows, set up with the sun to your back or angling over your shoulder so incoming birds will have a harder time seeing you.

Wade-in hunters should wear waders (as opposed to hip boots) to access deeper areas and for crossing gullies, beaver runs, etc. They should carry decoys and gear in a backpack or decoy bag with shoulder straps. Keep loads light by limiting the number of decoys or by using foam or inflatable decoys. A sling makes it easier to carry a shotgun, and a wading staff will help prevent falls or missteps into deep holes.

As in freelancing, fixed-blind hunting in swamps and marshes is a matter of choosing the right spot, and this can only be done through watching ducks work. Ferrying materials and building a permanent blind in a hard-to-reach spot are sweat-wrenching jobs, and you don't want to risk such effort on a chancy location. Do your homework first. Then you can enlarge or enhance the hole to make it more visible and attractive to passing ducks if you so desire.

Camouflage a permanent blind with the *same* type of materials as those growing around the hole, but cut them somewhere

else to keep from disturb-
ing the natural look of
the spot. The idea is to
blend the blind into the
landscape to as great a
degree as possible.
Sometimes it's better to
build a blind a few yards
back in the cover instead
of situating it at the edge
of the hole.

Building a fixed blind takes effort, so scout a location that's attractive to passing ducks.

Freelance or fixed-blind, hunting in swamps and marshes is
good until freezing weather arrives, and then it dies. Ice is the
shallow-water duck hunter's enemy. Ducks may stick around a
day or two after freeze-up, keeping "ice holes" open. But then
they will leave swamps and marshes for bigger water that's still
open (lakes, reservoirs, rivers), and they won't return until the
shallows thaw back out.

Hunting in Flooded Agricultural Fields

Each season, flooded grainfields provide some of the best
duck hunting in all four North American flyways. Some of these
fields are inundated naturally by heavy rains and resultant floods.
Others are flooded intentionally by catching or pumping in water
to cover crops grown specifically for attracting waterfowl. Corn,
rice, millet, milo, soybeans, and other grains rank high on dabbling ducks' list of preferred foods. Add shallow water to a field
with one of these crops, and the ducks will usually show up.

Most hunting in flooded grainfields is done from permanent blinds or pits. Many fields on hunting clubs or public wildlife management areas are flooded year after year, and best blind locations are learned through experience. For reasons known only to the ducks, they typically prefer to work one area of a flooded field better than others. Watch for this preference, then locate the blind accordingly.

This is where a floating blind has an advantage: it can be moved around. Sometimes ducks will "eat out" all the food in a particular area, then shift to another part of the field. When this happens, hunters can push or pull a floating blind to where the ducks are working and stay in the action.

Movable or fixed, a permanent blind in a field should have a low profile, and it should be totally covered with vegetation that's natural to the area.

Many hunters feel a pit is the best option for hiding in a flooded grainfield. A pit can be buried and concealed so it disappears from the landscape. Decoys can be set near the shooting hole so that ducks will work in closer. However, pits are obviously immovable, and a pit should only be set in a field after the site is proven. Bury a pit in the wrong spot, and you're stuck for the season.

© Bill Buckley

Permanent pit blinds offer the ultimate concealment in open fields.

One of the keys to success in hunting flooded fields is managing pressure. Unless new ducks are coming every day, a field that is hunted all day every day will get "burned out." The ducks will learn to avoid it because of the continual shooting.

More consistent shooting can be achieved by allowing the field to rest on certain days or portions of days. For instance, many clubs limit hunting to 2 to 4 days a week, resting their fields the other days. Or they may follow a restrictive hourly schedule, i.e., allowing shooting from 8 a.m. to 2 p.m. On such a schedule, ducks have periods when they can come into the field and feed without being harassed, and this helps ensure their continued use of the field.

Another way to manage pressure is to establish rest areas in certain flooded fields. (This obviously is possible only on clubs with enough land to set up their own mini-refuges.) Keep a concentration of ducks on the property, and some will invariably filter into the area where hunting is allowed.

One good idea when hunting flooded grainfields is to set out and pick up decoys each day. If decoys are left out continuously, ducks that come to feed during periods of no hunting will get used to them and know to avoid them. Keep decoys bagged up and stored in the blind. Then set them out at the beginning of each hunt according to wind direction. The ducks won't be used to seeing them and will react more naturally to them.

Also, flooded fields offer opportunity for freelance hunters, typically when rising water from a creek or river backs into adjacent bottomlands. Ducks frequently come in droves when this situation exists. Freelancers who locate a freshly flooded grainfield can have a bonanza of shooting!

When bottomlands along a creek or river are flooding, ducks will typically work the headwater area first, then follow the flood crest downstream. So when water starts dropping out of fields in the headwaters, freelancers should move progressively downstream with the birds.

The problem for freelancers in some flooded fields is how to get hidden. Many flooded fields are wide open, and it's easy for ducks to spot anything out of the ordinary. This is why freelancers must fashion some type of portable blind or do a good job of hiding in existing natural cover.

Sometimes simply crouching in a flooded cornfield will provide enough cover.

© Bill Buckley

Watch where ducks are working, then set up in the best cover closest to this center of activity. A gully, fencerow, tree line, clump of brush, or bulldozer pile might offer enough cover to conceal a boat blind or a hunter standing in the water. Take special care to use shadows and overhead cover, which are crucial to hiding from circling birds.

One effective freelance method for hiding in a flooded field is using a layout boat. This is a one-man shallow-draft boat that is towed to a selected spot and then camouflaged with natural materials. After setting out his decoys, a hunter climbs into his boat and lies flat on his back. Then he may cover his body with a net, piece of burlap, and/or natural cover (cornstalks, rice straw, etc.) A camo facemask, cap, and gloves provide the final touches for disappearing into the landscape.

I experimented with layout hunting several years back in an open Arkansas rice field. A cane blind in one side of the field stood out unnaturally, and all the ducks were working the other side. I waded into the field pulling a small fiber-glass layout boat that was loaded with decoys and camo net-ting. The ducks flushed at my approach, and I went straight to the area where they got up. I tossed out my decoys, then pulled the boat 30 yards upwind and set it with the bow wedged onto a rice levy to stabilize it. Then I covered the boat with the netting and rice straw. I climbed inside, lay back, spread a swatch of burlap to cover my upper body and shotgun, then waited for ducks to return. I had 4 greenheads in less than 30 minutes.

Another way to freelance in tall flooded crops—particu-larly corn—is to don waders, wade to where ducks are work-ing, then sit on a plastic bucket, stool, or folding chair to hide among the stalks. Wear camouflage with colors and patterns that match the natural cover, then simply hunker down and sit absolutely motionless while ducks are circling. This hunting method can be deadly on ducks that are shying away from fixed blinds in other parts of the field.

Jeff Baxter, Columbia, MO

"Concealment is What Kills Ducks"

Jeff Baxter is a freelance hunter who specializes in setting up in open areas where ducks are working and other hunters can't hide. "Concealment is what kills ducks," he says, "going where the ducks want to go and keeping a low profile and camouflaging with natural materials."

Specifically, Baxter uses a layout boat in some areas, covering it totally with natural grasses and brush, then climbing in and reclining. His profile height is only 18 inches above water or ground. Or if he's hunting in flooded standing corn, Baxter simply dons waders and sits on a folding stool amid the rows. "I lean over, hiding under the stalks and calling down toward the water. Of course, I wear camouflage that matches the vegetation in color and pattern. By doing this and staying rock-still while ducks are in close looking things over, I can work them right in with amazing consistency."

Hunting on Open Lakes, Reservoirs

Dabbling ducks routinely use big lakes and reservoirs for both feeding and resting, and these open waters offer a range of hunting opportunities. Many hunters freelance on big lakes. Others locate permanent blinds and decoy spreads in areas where ducks fly on a regular basis.

Hunting on big lakes and reservoirs can be "hot or cold." One day ducks may be abundant. The next day they can be scarce. Usually, the best times to hunt on open water are during a freeze, when shallow backwaters are locked up, and during a drought, when nearby shallows are dry. One of the least favorable times for hunting open water is after a heavy rain, when bottoms are flooding. Fresh, rising water and available new food lure ducks away from open lakes.

Hunting on open lakes and reservoirs usually gets better later in the season because of colder weather and ice buildup. Sometimes ducks collect on open water in huge concentrations, flying off the lake to feed in dry fields, then coming back in the midday to raft up and rest. Another good opportunity for hunting open water is during and immediately following a strong frontal passage. Big lakes and reservoirs can be magnets to newly arriving ducks.

Open-lake hunters should remember that dabbling ducks prefer shallow water, and this figures in choosing hunting sites. On big lakes and reservoirs, hunting for dabblers is usually better in headwater areas, backs of bays, shallow sides of points and islands, and other shallow, semi-protected areas. Wigeon, mallards, gadwall, and other species especially like to work shallow flats where aquatic vegetation is growing. Also, dabbling ducks will sometimes raft up in deep, wind-exposed areas, but this is more the exception than the rule.

In many respects, hunting on open lakes and reservoirs is similar to hunting on rivers. Some hunters freelance in boats or on the bank, setting up where they find birds. Other hunters locate fixed blinds under flight lanes or in known resting areas. Either of these methods can provide great shooting when conditions are good.

Freelancers should cover water and look for ducks. Sometimes they can do this by driving around the lakeshore. When they locate birds close to the bank or in the back of a bay or pocket, they can walk in, flush the ducks away, toss out a bag of decoys, and erect a portable blind or hide in available cover.

Shorelines can offer tremendous opportunities for fixed-blind hunters (above), and great potential for freelance hunters as well (below).

However, most freelancers hunt by boat, which gives them access to more territory. As on rivers, freelancers on big lakes should run and scout, then set up where they find ducks working or rafted up. They can hunt out of a boat blind, or they can stash the boat and hunt off the bank.

One advantage of this style of hunting is being able to adjust for different wind directions. Dabbling ducks like to hang out in areas where they are sheltered from the wind. These areas vary from day to day as wind direction shifts. Thus freelancers might have success one day on one side of an island or point, then better luck the next day on the other side due to a wind change. Regardless, let the ducks tell you where they want to be. Don't try to force them to work somewhere they'd prefer not to be.

Decoy visibility is important on open water, so oversized decoys are better than standards. Magnums and super magnums can be seen farther by ducks on the wing. Black duck and/or pintail decoys will add to a spread's long distance visibility. Also, the more decoys a freelancer can deploy the better, and one or two spinning-wing decoys are super effective at attracting passing ducks' attention.

One especially deadly strategy for freelancing on open lakes is to hunt around "inside points" during a hard freeze or blow. An inside point is the back, wind-protected side of a point that juts into the main body of a lake. When ducks are returning to open water after feeding, many times they will follow the main shoreline, looking for a resting spot. When they fly past a point, hear calling and look and see decoys, it's easy for them to curl around and land. It's a convenient ambush.

The easiest way for hunters to find a good inside point is—again—to run close to shore and watch where ducks get up. Then they should toss out decoys where the birds flushed, stash the boat, and hide in natural cover or a temporary blind erected on the bank.

Open lakes and reservoirs also provide tremendous opportunity for fixed-blind hunters. Throughout North America, floating, stake, or permanent bank blinds rule over bays, open water flats, chutes between islands, and other areas where ducks feed, rest, or travel on a regular basis.

For hunting dabbling ducks, a permanent blind should be located in relatively shallow water. If possible, it should be in an area that is sheltered from prevailing winds. It should be totally covered with camouflage materials, since it will be wide open to ducks' scrutiny.

Floating blinds are a good option (albeit a more expensive one) for hunting on open water. A floating blind may be moved to match changes in ducks' flight patterns. It may be turned to correspond with different winds. It will ride up and down with water-level fluctuations. It can be removed at season's end for repair and re-camouflaging before the next season.

Many fixed-blind hunters on open water set out huge, permanent decoy spreads to resemble a raft of resting waterfowl. Such spreads—sometimes numbering in the hundreds of decoys—have a strong persuasive effect on ducks passing overhead. They also require great effort and constant attention to deploy and keep looking natural—no tangles.

A prime time for hunting rivers is late in the season, after other bodies of water have frozen.

Chapter Two

Hunting on Rivers

Navigable rivers flow throughout the U.S. and Canada, and collectively they offer one of the greatest, least-used resources for duck hunting. Before the days of refuges and reservoirs, rivers were the primary holding areas for waterfowl. Today, large numbers of ducks and geese still use these waterways both as migration corridors and as stopovers for feeding and resting. But since most hunters now focus on refuges, reservoirs, management areas, and other more accessible hunting locations, hunting pressure on rivers is usually light.

Rivers are the domain of the freelancer. The main technique for hunting on them is running in boats and scouting for ducks. When a concentration is located, river hunters can set up where and as they wish. Rivers are wild and free, and so is the hunting on them.

Veteran river runners know there are times and conditions when hunting on rivers is better. One such time is when water levels are rising and backing into fields and timber in adjacent bottomlands. A flood makes fresh food readily available, and ducks pour in for the banquet. They can show up overnight to take advantage of a new feeding opportunity.

Another good time to hunt on rivers is during a hard freeze. Rivers will remain open long after shallow, calm waters are frozen. Dabbling ducks will hang around an area several days after a freeze hits. These birds will usually feed in dry grainfields early in the morning and late in the afternoon, and they will loaf on a river during midday. They will hang out in eddy pockets, creek mouths, and similar spots where current is slack and staying put is easy.

A third good time to hunt on rivers is during a drought. Again, the ducks are on rivers out of necessity. When shallow swamps and marshes dry up, ducks go where they can find water. During a drought, the water level on a river is usually low, exposing mud flats, sand bars, and other "structure" that attracts the birds. Again, ducks will rest in eddies, sloughs, ponds on sandbars, and other shallow waterholes sheltered from currents and winds.

River hunters must be prospectors. They should motor up creeks and sloughs that empty into the river. They should check chutes behind islands, eddies behind jetties, backwaters breaking into river bottoms, *anywhere* they can maneuver their boat where ducks might be found. Their goal is to observe ducks going into a spot or to flush birds off the water. Then they set up there and wait for more ducks to come.

This type of hunting requires very specialized equipment. Boats for running rivers should be large and seaworthy enough to ferry heavy loads of hunters, decoys, and gear through dangerous waters. Rivers can get rough, especially when a strong wind is blowing against the current. Also, river hunters may encounter barge wakes, floating logs, ice floes, and other hazards. This is why venturing onto a large river in a small, low-sided boat is risky business. Don't do it! A 16-foot deep-V boat or high-sided johnboat should be the minimum used in river hunting.

A river-running boat's outboard must have enough horsepower to push the boat fast enough to cover long stretches of river when looking for ducks. Sometimes hunters will run miles before setting up. The boat should also be equipped with a high-volume bilge pump in case the boat springs a leak or takes a wave over the bow. It should have proper running lights and a spotlight for night running.

River hunters must have some system for camouflaging the boat and themselves once a hunting site is selected. A portable blind attached to the boat is the best, most convenient solution to this problem. Also, hunters can use a combination of camo netting, tarps, and natural cover to fashion a makeshift blind.

Boat blinds offer concealment on the go.

Once again, safety cannot be overemphasized when it comes to river hunting. Big rivers are wild places where help usually isn't immediately available. A swamped boat, a boat that drifts away, a hole in the hull, an outboard that won't start, or another similar dilemma can get serious in a hurry. Don't take chances. Always wear personal flotation devices when river running. Carry survival gear—such as extra clothes, a fire starting kit, signal flares, tools, food, etc—in a dry bag. And always tell someone where you're going and when you plan to return. This way, if you're stranded on a river, rescuers will know where to look.

Hunting from a fixed blind is also an option on rivers. A floating blind is the best alternative, since it can be towed to the chosen spot, and a floating blind will ride up and down with fluctuating water levels.

A floating blind might be positioned on an island point or chute, creek mouth, flat, or other spot where ducks frequently pass over or work in. Pay special attention to how the blind is secured. Perhaps the best way is to use steel cable or strong ropes to tie it to trees or other stationary objects on the riverbank or in the water. It's difficult to anchor a blind in current where strong winds and/or floods are likely to move it sometime during the season. If anchors must be used, leave plenty slack in the lines to allow for water fluctuations.

On rivers, most fixed-blind hunters usually set out and pick up their decoys each day. Decoys left for extended periods are subject to loss to strong currents, debris washing through the spread, high water, etc. Some hunters in quiet backwaters leave big decoy spreads out through the season. However, if any current is present, take the decoys in when you leave. This will probably "save their lives."

Hunting in Flooded Timber

For many duck hunters, this is the epitome of their sport. Hiding behind a tree, kicking water, and working mallards down through the forest canopy is an old standard in waterfowling. This type of hunting is most prevalent in mid- and lower Mississippi Flyway states, particularly Arkansas, Mississippi, Tennessee, and northern Louisiana.

Much flooded timber hunting is done on private clubs where hardwood tracts are levied and water is pumped in in fall and winter. Freelancers get their turn on wildlife management areas and low-country rivers that flood seasonally and back out into adjoining hardwood forests. In mallard country, when water rises in green timber, these ducks usually pour in to feed on acorns, weed seeds, and invertebrates as well as to rest in the quiet sanctuary of the woods. Ducks work into flooded timber better on sunny days than on cloudy days. On cloudy days they are more skittish, and since there are no shadows, it's easier for them to spy hunters trying to hide in the woods below.

This type of hunting can be both intimidating and confusing to hunters who lack experience in flooded timber. When the Mississippi, Ohio, White, Cache, Yazoo, and other major rivers back out, they inundate low-lying forests that cover hundreds

© Bill Buckley

In flooded timber hunting, the trick is locating where the ducks will be on a given day.

DeWitt Nixon, Jacksonville, AR

"Stilking" in Flooded Timber

DeWitt Nixon has hunted on Arkansas's Bayou Meto wildlife area (near Stuttgart) for 40 years. Bayou Meto is one of the best green timber reservoirs in the nation, spanning some 34,000 acres and attracting clouds of mallards when water conditions are good.

This area is also known for heavy shooting pressure from crowds of hunters, and Nixon says ducks quickly become educated by this pounding. "They start avoiding the obvious holes and open woods, and they begin working in 'thickety areas' where there's better cover and less pressure."

Nixon continues, "Ducks usually hit these spots in small groups—typically 5 to 15 birds. They'll come down through the smallest opening in the forest canopy. Then they'll swim out into the brush where they can spend the day without being harassed."

Nixon hunts these reticent ducks by "stilking" through the timber. "Stilking" is a hybrid word that he coined—a combination of "still-hunting" and "stalking."

He explains, "You watch which way the ducks are flying, and you wade through the woods in that direction. You just cover ground until you find that little overlooked area where there are ducks but no hunters."

Nixon says when a hunter gets close to where he sees ducks going down, it's time to get stealthy. "If you're good at slipping, you can ease right up on ducks on the water and get a jump shot."

When "stilking," Nixon wears full camo, including headnet and gloves. He explains that minimal disturbance is essential in this ease-along style of hunting. He moves ever so slowly, making absolutely no sloshing noises and as few ripples as possible. When he can, he wades with the sun at his back, and he sticks to the shadows of the trees. He cradles his shotgun in his arms, and he never fidgets or makes sudden, impulsive movements. "It's hard to emphasize how much you must concentrate, how slow you must go, and how quiet you must be. One little finger movement or head turn can blow the whole deal. But if you're patient and quiet and totally focused, you can consistently slip close enough to resting ducks to get a jump shot."

and sometimes thousands of acres. How can a hunter find ducks in these giant mazes of trees and brush? How can he get to them? How can he keep from getting lost?

Locating ducks in green timber is like pinpointing bass or crappie in a lake. On any given day, 90 percent of the ducks will be using 10 percent of the area. The trick is finding the right 10 percent, which will change from day to day according to water levels, availability of food, and gunning pressure. If water is rising, most ducks will go to that part of the woods that's the shallowest and most freshly flooded. Just a few inches of water are plenty for ducks to find food and resting sanctuary. Also, sustained hunting pressure will cause ducks to shift to other areas where pressure is not so heavy.

This is why hunters in flooded timber must be mobile and able to follow ducks as they move around. They should use a flat-bottom johnboat (a semi-V is best since it glances off trees) and a shallow-draft motor to run creeks, sloughs, dredge ditches, flooded roads, and other trails through the woods, all the while watching where ducks are going and heading in their direction. When hunters can no longer run their boat they should tie it to a tree and continue wading toward where ducks are going down.

But don't leave the boat without taking a fix with a GPS (global positioning system). This handy navigational device is a godsend for hunters in flooded timber. With a GPS and the knowledge of how to use it, a hunter will never be lost (as long as his batteries are fresh). He can store a fix for his boat, truck, honey hole, whatever. Then the "Go To" arrow will always point the direction to the waypoint he selects.

If a hunter doesn't have a GPS, he should carry a compass and take note of landmarks that can help him find his way back to his starting point. Some hunters carry orange survey tape and flag their trail as they wade in. This system works well, but they should always remove the flags on their way out.

The simple point is, it's very easy to get disoriented in flooded timber, particularly on cloudy days. Hunters heading into strange woods should be aware of this danger and be diligent about using a GPS, compass, flags, or whatever to keep from getting lost.

Wading through flooded timber is easier if hunters have special equipment for doing so. A sling makes toting a shotgun more convenient. A neoprene waist belt is handy for carrying shells. A wading staff will provide insurance against tripping on tree roots, stumps, and holes hidden beneath the water. And if a hunter desires to tote in decoys, a backpack or decoy bag with shoulder straps is a necessity. (Many green timber veterans forgo using decoys and depend, instead, on calling and kicking water to lure ducks in.)

The best advice in this regard is to keep the load light. Hunters may wind up wading several hundred yards to get to the right spot. Too heavy a burden will make this trek all the more difficult, and it will increase the likelihood of falling and getting wet. A dozen standard-size decoys is a good load for one hunter. Or consider investing in soft foam or inflatable rubber decoys that weigh almost nothing, then you can pack in as many as you wish.

When hunters reach the area where ducks are working in flooded timber, they must decide where to set their decoys. Most timber hunting veterans will look for an opening or break in the woods, however slight, which offers ducks an easier descent. A "hole" might be a natural gap or where a tree has fallen over, or it might even be a place where the canopy is thinner.

When a hunting spot is selected and decoys are set out (see chapter 4 for details), hunters retreat a few yards back into the woods on the upwind or crosswind side of the hole, and each person picks a tree to hide behind, preferably in the trunk's shadow. When ducks are working, hunters hug their trees, kick water to produce ripples, and chuckle or call as the situation dictates.

Safety is a primary concern when hunting in flooded timber. Hunters should pick shooting spots in a line on the same side of the hole, and each hunter should acknowledge his own zone of fire. When ducks come in and the shooting starts, the birds will scatter, and it takes discipline on each hunter's part to keep this situation from becoming dangerous.

While wading and "hugging a tree" is the standard method for hunting in flooded timber, much hunting is also done from boat blinds and permanent blinds. Boat blinds are very convenient when the water is deep enough and the woods thin enough to maneuver the boat to where ducks are working. The boat will haul decoys and gear, and the blind will offer full concealment.

One special opportunity in flooded timber comes when a hard freeze locks up still, shallow flats. Sometimes, current in creek channels and dredge ditches may keep ice from forming in adjacent woods. Such an area is like a magnet to ducks. Hunters who can find and access open water in the middle of a frozen woods can have a field day.

Permanent blinds characteristically rule over proven holes in flooded timber. They offer the ultimate in convenience: boat in, climb into the blind, load shotguns, and start the coffee. However, the disadvantage of hunting from a permanent blind is the obvious lack of options if the ducks aren't working that area. When ducks fail to show, permanent blind hunters who don't have a freelance capability are doomed to have a slow day.

Hunting in Dry Fields

In fall and winter, dabbling ducks frequently feed in dry grainfields. I've hunted ducks in dry fields in all three of

In a dry cornfield, a chair can make the waiting easier.

Canada's Prairie Provinces, in North and South Dakota, Kentucky, and Arkansas. In all these places, the birds' patterns have been similar. They fly out from their rest areas at first light for an early-morning feeding period, then they feed in the fields again in late afternoon. Hunters who are set up in the right location when the ducks arrive can enjoy exceptional shooting.

Three main factors come into play when hunting ducks in dry fields: finding the exact spot where ducks are feeding ("spotting"), setting out a realistic decoy spread, and hiding in the wide open spaces of a harvested field.

When feeding in a grainfield, ducks tend to work the same area until all the grain is depleted. This means they will frequently return to the same exact spot in the morning after feeding there in the afternoon, or vice versa. This is why hunters must do a thorough job of scouting, not just finding the field where ducks are working, but pinpointing the precise location *in the field* where the birds are feeding, then setting up there.

Standard procedure for a morning hunt is to drive backroads the afternoon before and watch for ducks funneling into a field. When a concentration is located, move in closer and take a fix on where they are feeding. Mark it visually and mentally so you can return to it the next morning in the predawn darkness. (Then, if you don't have hunting permission, go find the landowner and ask for his go-ahead.)

The next morning, return to this spot far enough ahead of dawn to set out your decoys and arrange your blinds or dig pits.

Goose decoys can increase the visibility and drawing power of a dry-field spread.

Decoy spreads for field hunting are typically large, for both their visibility to ducks and concealment for hunters. Many ducks are taken over goose decoys (full-bodies, shells, and silhouettes). Goose decoys are larger and more visible than duck decoys. Many hunters set a core of goose decoys, then supplement their spread with duck decoys around the edges and in the shooting area. Duck shells and silhouettes are most popular with field hunters. Full-body standup duck decoys in key locations in the spread add a convincing touch of realism.

One special decoy set for dry field hunting involves swatches of black roofing paper scattered over the ground. Details of this system are provided in chapter 4.

When setting decoys in a dry field, pay close attention to wind direction and arrange the spread accordingly. Many hunters set decoys in a shallow U formation facing directly downwind. Ducks work into the opening, between the two arms and head-on toward hunters lined up along the base of the U. If the spread is skewed just slightly from straight downwind, the ducks will come in at an angle, and one or two hunters on that end of the line will get all the shooting.

Hiding in a dry field spread can be accomplished by simply lying prone in the decoys, by using layout blinds, by digging and hiding in shallow pits, or by using a hay roll blind or some other portable blind.

Lying prone in the decoys works well if the spread is large enough for hunters to blend in. If the ground is damp, take a waterproof pad to lie on. Many field hunters also use a grass mat or square of burlap or camo material to cover themselves. A facemask is a good idea. And another very helpful accessory is some type of support that slightly elevates and supports the upper back and head. This aids in watching downwind for incoming birds and also for rising up to shoot.

Layout blinds are extremely effective and popular in field hunting. A layout blind is like a mobile above-ground pit. A hunter can position it where he wishes, add a little natural camouflage, then climb in and disappear. Hunters shoot from layout blinds lined up a few yards apart in the decoys. Ducks pay little attention to these "bumps" in the spread.

Digging individual pits is an option for field hunting, but not a very good one. Pitting in is a lot of work. Also, if the ducks aren't working your spot, all the effort has been wasted. You can't pick pits up and move them. Additionally, many farmers don't like holes dug in their fields. (Pits should always be completely filled in and packed down when a hunt is completed.)

In summary, field hunting for ducks can be as spectacular and exciting as this sport gets. Ducks normally work dry fields in large flights. They come into a well-set spread with little hesitation, sometimes landing on the ground right in front of you. In such a case, safety should always be foremost in every shooter's mind. Talk about zones of fire before the action begins, then strictly enforce them when the birds start showing up.

Float-Hunting

Float-hunting involves floating in a boat down a free-flowing river or creek and shooting ducks that flush or pass overhead. This hunting method is not widely practiced, but not because it is ineffective. Indeed, float-hunting can be a very productive, enjoyable, adventuresome alternative to more-standard hunting methods. Also, since most streams and rivers in the U.S. are public, float-hunting is a viable option for hunters who don't have access or the means to hunt more traditional areas.

Float-hunting is most effective during freezes when ponds and swamps are iced over and ducks are forced to relocate to flowing waters. Another good time to float-hunt is during a drought, when shallow areas are dry (assuming there's still enough flow in the stream to make an easy transition). Conversely, float-hunting is poorest during warm, high water conditions when dabbling ducks are attracted to shallow, still waters and fresh food sources.

A float-hunt is usually conducted by two hunters working together. One vehicle is left at a take-out point, then the boat(s) and second vehicle are ferried to some point upstream where the float begins.

Gun in one hand, paddle in the other, this float hunter attempts to sneak into shooting range of swimming ducks.

Hunters can float-hunt in any of several types of boats, but two work best. The first is a canoe. A canoe is silent, highly maneuverable, and plenty stable for float-hunting. (A fiberglass or ABF plastic canoe is much quieter and better for float-hunting than an aluminum canoe.) The shooter rides in the front, shotgun ready, and the paddler sits in back, controlling the canoe's speed and track. A canoe used in float-hunting should be painted camo color or camouflaged with net and natural brush, vines, etc. A red canoe won't work!

The second good choice for float-hunting is a Poke Boat, made by Phoenix Poke Boats, Inc., of Berea, Kentucky. The Poke Boat looks like a kayak but has a flat-bottom design and much greater stability than a traditional kayak. Poke Boats come in one- and two-man models. Poke Boats are constructed from high-grade fiberglass or Kevlar. They are extremely tough and lightweight (22 pounds for the one-man model, 46 pounds for the two-man model). They are also highly maneuverable, draft mere inches with a full load, and have a low profile. A Poke Boat used for float-hunting should also be painted in camouflage colors.

Some hunters float in a johnboat, but this is a poor choice because of its noisiness and lack of maneuverability. A johnboat's aluminum construction magnifies every bump and scrape, and this type of boat is far more difficult to paddle downstream than a canoe or Poke Boat. A johnboat's best application in float-hunting is on a larger stream where an electric motor (mounted on the back) can be used.

A float-hunt entails floating downstream while watching for ducks on the water or flying above. Mallards, wood ducks, black ducks, and other dabblers like to loaf in eddy pockets or in long straight stretches where current is light. Frequently these ducks will perch on logs or sandbars to preen and rest after feeding.

As they float or paddle downstream, hunters should be dressed in full camo, including face mask and gloves. They should be as silent and still as possible. The idea is to be unidentifiable as humans to ducks and to appear instead as logs or other debris washing down-current.

One good tip is to affix some leafy oak branches, cane, or other natural brush to a boat's bow to screen hunters from ducks' view. A small amount of brush wired, tied, or taped onto the front of the boat will provide a much more natural look and cause ducks to be less suspicious of the object floating in their direction.

On long straight stretches, when hunters spy ducks ahead on the water, they should remain motionless and drift with the current. Ducks may become anxious about the strange object heading their way, but if they aren't threatened or alarmed they won't usually flush. Instead, they will start swimming downstream, keeping a safe distance between them and the unidentified intruder.

Eventually, they will tire of being herded downstream, and they will also lose some of their caution about the strange object following them. When this happens, the ducks will swim into an eddy or behind a log or a bend in the channel. Then they will hide and wait for the intruder to go past them.

This gives float-hunters a chance to close within shotgun range. The paddler keeps the boat pointed forward by sculling on the side opposite the ducks. (The canoe and the paddler's hunched-over body screen the sculling motion from the birds' view.) Then, when close enough to shoot, the shooter raises up, flushes the ducks, and takes his toll.

Another tactic when float-hunting is to hug the inside of all channel turns, hoping to surprise ducks idling in eddies on the downstream side of the turns. The shooter should remain alert and ready to shoot in an instant. Frequently ducks will flush unexpectedly next to the bank or from behind cover.

A third float-hunting tactic is to spot ducks downstream and scull out of their view. The shooter then disembarks and circles on land to get ahead of the ducks. When he's had time to complete this maneuver, the second hunter resumes paddling and herds the ducks down to his partner's ambush.

Float-hunters should keep gear to a minimum: shells, call, chemical hand warmers, food, a thermos of coffee. Also, floaters might carry a half-dozen foam decoys rolled up and stuffed in the bow of the boat. This way, if they find a slough or flat where ducks are working, they can set the decoys out, hide the boat, and hunt off the bank.

Safety is always *the main consideration* in float-hunting. Each float-hunter should wear a Coast Guard-certified life vest or float coat. (A waist belt or CO_2-inflatable vest is recommended because of its lack of bulk.) Also, roll a canoe and get wet on a cold day, and hypothermia can set in quickly. This is why each float-hunter should carry a fire starting kit in a waterproof packet on his body. Then, if an unexpected wetting occurs, a fire can be built to ward off what could become a serious emergency.

Jump-Shooting

Jump-shooting is what its name describes: locating ducks on the water, stalking up close, then shooting them on the flush. This is another hunting method that is seldom practiced but which can be both productive and fun when seriously pursued.

When stalking ducks, the jump-shooter must move slowly and deliberately.

The first step in jump-shooting is finding ducks, and a hunter may accomplish this in several ways. He can drive backroads and check ponds and potholes with binoculars. Then, when he spots birds, he can vacate his vehicle and make a stalk.

He can walk or wade through marshes and swamps, looking for ducks on the water or working into a given area. Again, when he locates birds he can plan his stalk according to the cover and prevailing wind.

A third way to jump-shoot is to slip along a creek or river, peeping over the bank every hundred yards or so and scanning for ducks. When he spots some, a hunter can ease away from the bank, circle, then move in abreast of the birds for the shot.

Stalking ducks is similar to slipping up on other game. Movements should be slow and deliberate. Hunters should study their approach carefully and use terrain features, shadows, and natural cover to conceal their advance. Jump-shooters should dress in full camouflage, including face mask and gloves. Also, a shotgun with a camo or black matte finish is better, since there's no glint from shiny metal.

Pass-shooting

Pass-shooting is perhaps the simplest form of duck hunting. A hunter merely positions himself beneath ducks' flight path and fires at birds winging overhead. Pass-shooting may take place on a flyway between feeding and resting areas, between two rest ponds, along a refuge boundary, on the point of an island, or any similar spot over or close to which ducks predictably fly.

The challenges come in finding such a place, then being able to bag birds at maximum ranges. Hunters wishing to try pass-shooting must be observant of ducks' flight patterns and set up accordingly. They should also realize that pass-shooting is generally better in low-sky, high-wind conditions, when ducks characteristically fly lower. Pass-shooting can be a washout on clear, no-wind or low-wind days when ducks fly higher. Also, special pass-shooting opportunities exist when shooting time approaches in the morning and just before it goes out in the afternoon. Ducks normally fly closer to the ground during these low light periods.

When pass-shooting, hunters must exercise good judgment and ethics in deciding which shots to take. Trying shots that are too far can lead to crippling and the wasteful loss of unrecovered birds. Pass-shooters should test the range capabilities of their guns and loads, then not take shots longer than those at which they're able to make clean kills. For instance, with a 3½-

inch 12-gauge shooting steel BBs the maximum range is approximately 50 yards. With heavier non-toxic loads such as Remington Hevi-Shot, Bismuth No-Tox, Kent Impact TungstenMatrix, and Federal Tungsten-Iron the range will be lengthened another 5 to 10 yards.

Some hunters take advantage of terrain features to position themselves closer to waterfowl flying overhead. I've hunted a bluff overlooking South Dakota's Lake Oahe, where Canada geese and occasional mallards fly "uphill" en route to this region's cornfields. As they crest over the top, they frequently pass within range of hunters hiding in pits dug into the edge of the bluff. I once shot from a hilltop in Nebraska over which ducks were passing en route from one lake to another. And I've seen (though not sampled) a shooting platform built in the top of a tall cypress tree on Reelfoot Lake in west Tennessee. When that platform is occupied, ducks flying low over the timber are in for a rude awakening.

Hunting During Special Teal/Wood Duck Seasons

Early duck seasons offer special, bonus opportunities for hunters to bag teal and—in three states—wood ducks. Blue-winged teal, especially, migrate south well before other dabbling duck species. Most leave northern breeding/nesting areas by early to mid-September, and are long gone to wintering grounds on the southern coast and in Central and South America by the time regular duck seasons come in. So to use this resource, hunters are allowed an early teal season before the regular duck season opens. This season typically lasts two weeks in September. The bag limit in recent years has been 4 teal daily (combination of species).

In addition, hunters in Kentucky, Tennessee, and Florida are allowed two wood ducks in their 4-bird early-duck-season bag. (To mitigate this bonus, early seasons in these states are shortened to five days.) Many woodies are produced on streams and sloughs in these states, and like teal, these ducks have mostly migrated south by the time regular

A few states allow two wood ducks as part of the early-season bag.

duck seasons open. The early season thus provides hunters with a chance at these wood ducks while they're still present. (Research studies have shown that the harvest of teal and wood ducks during the early season has little impact on overall numbers of these species over the long term.)

There are two keys to success during the early duck season: scouting and timing. Scouting is enormously important in locating both teal and wood ducks. When stopping over during migration, teal will frequent marshes, potholes in mud flats, river oxbows, farm ponds, beaver ponds, and other quiet, shallow waters. Wood ducks will share many of these same locations, and they particularly like the backs of coves on big reservoirs.

The time to scout is just prior to opening day. Teal, especially, can be here today and gone tomorrow. Locate a concentration a week before the season comes in, then go back on opening morning and the birds may have departed. Instead, it's best to scout—or to recheck a spot—a day or two before opening day. Then, if ducks are present and there's no weather frontal activity in the forecast, it's a safe bet that the birds will still be there on opening morning.

When the season is in progress, a new wave of migrating teal will likely come on each frontal push. Teal hunters should watch local weather reports and go hunting during, or the morning after, a cold front's passage, however slight. If you hit the migration right, the number of new teal showing up on a lake or pond can be dramatic.

Years ago, two friends and I were hunting during the teal season on a lake in Kentucky. There were a few bluewings around, but shooting had been sporadic. But by 8 a.m. what had been a southerly wind shifted to the north and a bank of high clouds moved in. Suddenly teal began showing up in droves. Every 10 minutes a new flight averaging 30 to 50 birds would appear, and they'd dive bomb our decoys. We bagged our limits in short order. This was as spectacular a migration in progress as I've ever witnessed in duck hunting.

Once located, teal and wood ducks are relatively easy to hunt. Show up before dawn to toss out decoys and, if necessary, to build a temporary blind. Large spreads aren't necessary. If the spot is right, one to two dozen decoys will be plenty. I use mallard hen decoys. Some hunters use teal decoys, but mallards are larger and more easily seen by flying ducks. Also, I use hens because ducks haven't attained mating plumage in September. Their colors are still drab, so the all-brown decoys look more natural.

Any type of blind—natural or artificial—will work if the cover is thick enough. Cattails, reeds, buck bushes, willows, logs, and other vegetation offer plenty concealment. Bring a plastic bucket to sit on, and use a machete or hatchet to cut brush to thicken the blind as needed. Camo netting or other screening materials may also be used. If possible, arrange your decoys and blind so you're sitting with the sun at your back or side.

Hunting this early duck season is a bonus, and it's a good tune-up for later seasons. Shooting can be surprisingly consistent for hunters who put in the effort to locate teal and, where legal, wood ducks. This is a good outing for young hunters and young retrievers, since the weather is generally warm and the hunt easy.

Dealing with Hunting Pressure

Throughout the U.S., many hunters pursue dabbling ducks on public waterfowl areas where competition from other hunters is heavy. In this case, their success often hinges not only on their hunting skills, but also on their ability to work around—or escape—the crowds.

In such a situation, and when possible, freelance hunters should try to find areas where pressure is less. This might be a spot where ducks aren't as numerous, but the birds that are there are able to work. They aren't continually called to and shot at by other hunters. It doesn't take clouds of ducks to make a good hunt. Just a few in the right spot and frame of mind are plenty to provide a generous bag.

When shotguns are booming, ducks frequently shy away to places where cover is thicker and the disturbance factor is less. In swamps, marshes, flooded timber, etc., they will circle and search until they find an area where they can land and rest undisturbed. Then ducks on the water will draw more ducks, and this is how a concentration builds up.

Freelance hunters find these spots by being mobile and doing a thorough job of scouting. They follow ducks by boat and on foot, trying to locate an area that other hunters have overlooked, or that others won't work hard enough to reach. There's a lot of sweat equity in such an effort, but the payoff comes in the satisfaction of finding ducks that other hunters don't know about.

A few seasons back a friend and I were hunting on a public area where ducks were plentiful, but pressure was heavy. Several other parties were scattered around us; nobody was having much luck. Anytime a flight got close, several callers would call, and when a duck dropped below 60 yards, skybusters would open up.

My partner noticed a flight of mallards working down behind a tree line several hundred yards from where we were set up. A few minutes later another flight went into the same area, and a third flight followed after a short time.

That was all we needed to see. We picked up our decoys and waded back to the boat. I retrieved an area map that I kept in the dry box. After a few minutes of map study we had a new game

Chapter Two

Allen Hughes, Memphis, TN

"Etiquette For Hunting in a Crowd"

Allen Hughes frequently hunts on popular waterfowl management areas in Tennessee, Arkansas, and Mississippi, and he says sometimes crowds are heavy and competition for ducks is fierce. Hughes says this can lead some hunters to act selfishly and to disregard others' rights. He stresses that if hunters are respectful and courteous to others, everyone will enjoy their hunt more, and will probably experience greater success.

Following is a collective list of dos and don'ts for hunting in a crowd.

1. Don't squeeze in on other hunters. Respect their space.

2. Don't pass-shoot at ducks that are swinging somebody else's decoys.

3. Don't try to call ducks away from another party when they're locked onto their spread.

4. If moving through an area and another party is working ducks, stop or do whatever is necessary to avoid flaring their birds.

5. Don't speak derogatorily about nearby hunters. Sound travels well over water, and under-the-breath criticisms could escalate competitive tensions.

6. Stay in line and wait your turn at the boat ramp.

7. Don't block the boat ramp. Be loaded and ready to launch when your turn comes.

8. When trailering your boat, clear the ramp quickly. Wait to store gear and fasten tie-down straps until you're out of the way.

9. When running a boat, be courteous with your wake when passing other boats or wading hunters.

10. If you finish your limit, pick up and leave quickly so others can claim your spot.

11. Ultimately, remember the Golden Rule and apply it when hunting. By treating other hunters fairly and respectfully, you will have a more enjoyable, less stressful hunt, and hopefully the example you set will have a positive influence on other parties in the area.

plan. We'd run the boat around an island, park it, and walk up the tree line where we'd seen the ducks going.

After an hour of motoring, walking, and wading, we pushed into a brushy area with a couple of open beaver ponds. More than a hundred mallards and gadwall flushed! We'd backpacked in a dozen decoys, which we quickly tossed out where the real birds had been sitting. Then we hid in nearby cover and waited for the next flight. When we left a couple of hours later, we were two ducks short of filling our double limit.

Freelance hunters have the mobility to search out new places when ducks move in response to changes in water/feeding conditions.

A second strategy for hunting on crowded areas is to avoid weekends and go on weekdays when hunter numbers should be fewer. Also, many public areas are closed on specified days to try to keep ducks around. Usually, hunting on an area is better the first day after hunting has been closed for a couple of days (i.e., if an area has been closed Monday and Tuesday, go hunting on Wednesday).

A third strategy is to "take second helpings." Don't show up early and fight the predawn crowds. Instead, plan to arrive on site an hour or so after shooting time, then move into a good spot or blind after a party finishes their hunt and comes out. Many public areas specify that blinds are open on a first-come, first-served basis after shooting hours start. Be first in line after a party limits out or quits hunting, and you could be a double winner. You get to sleep late, and you still get in a quality hunt.

Many public areas allow hunting from fixed blinds only, and the blinds are close enough where hunters compete against each other for working ducks. In this situation, common courtesy should be the standard among competitors. If ducks are working another hunter's spread, stay off the call and let him have them. Then, if they swing away from his blind, they're fair game. Too often, overzealous competition and resultant hard feelings spoil an experience that is meant to be fun.

Having said this, there are several tricks a hunter can employ to pull more ducks his way in this situation. Bigger decoy spreads usually draw more attention from airborne birds. Use lots of motion in the spread—wing-spinners, jerk strings, etc. Use magnum decoys or Canada geese for better visibility. I like black decoys mixed throughout a spread for the same purpose. Callers should use loud, high-pitched calls, and two or more callers should call together to gain and *hold ducks' attention*. This last phrase is the key to hunting in a competitive setting. Once you get ducks' attention, try to keep it by continuing to double-call, mixing in feed calls and not letting up until it's time to shoot. If circling ducks begin drifting away toward another caller, call loudly and emphatically to suck them back your way. (Refer to chapters 3 and 4 for more detail about calling and decoy strategies.)

Above everything else, location probably has more to do with success in a competitive situation than any other factor. If you're where the ducks want to go, it'll be hard to keep them away. If you're where they *don't* want to go, it'll be hard to make them come. Even with the best decoy spread, calling, and blind, the most important factor is location. When possible, go where ducks are trying to work, and get ready to shoot.

Chapter Three

How to Call Dabbling Ducks

The lone duck was just a speck in the sky, several hundred yards across the swamp from our blind. He wasn't flying the straight line of a bird that knew where he was going. Instead, he was veering back and forth as though searching for a landing spot. He looked like he might respond to a call, but he was so far away.

"I'm going to call that duck," I said to my partner with a hint of swagger. No other birds were in sight, and I had nothing to lose in trying to hail this one.

My buddy snickered, "He'll never hear you at that distance."

"I think he *can* hear me. I'll *make* him hear me," I boasted.

I had a couple of aces up my sleeve. First, a gusty wind was blowing in the duck's direction. I knew that calling carries much farther downwind than upwind or on no wind at all.

And second, I had my Reelfoot Lake-style call in my shell bag. It has a large wooden barrel and a metal reed. It's designed for high pitch and loud volume that carry over long distances. I don't normally blow this call at this hunting spot, since ducks are usually in close here, and "power calling" isn't necessary. However, in this instance it was my only hope.

I fetched the call from the bag, drew in a full breath, and commenced blowing. I started with one long, extended note, then followed with several loud, fast staccato notes that are characteristic of the Reelfoot highball. *Taaaaa... ta, ta, ta, ta, ta, ta, ta, ta, ta,*

and on and on until I ran out of air. Then I refilled my lungs and started over. Two series, three. There was nothing natural-sounding about this style of calling, but I knew from experience that if the duck could hear it, there was a chance he'd respond.

Use large-barreled, Reelfoot Lake-style calls to bring in distant ducks.

Suddenly the bird veered my way. "He's got it," I said, sucking in still another breath.

"No way," my partner rebutted.

But the duck *did* have it. I poured the calling at him, and he locked on like an airplane following a radio beacon.

"I can't believe this!" my friend muttered. I kept blowing.

In a matter of seconds the lone greenhead had spotted our decoys, arched his wings, and started to glide. I toned down the volume but kept up the fast-paced rhythm. The duck was coming as though hypnotized. No need to change now!

The drake never circled. Instead, he sailed straight in and flared over the open hole in the middle of our spread. "Take him. You deserve him," my partner whispered. I was glad to oblige.

In four decades of passionate duck hunting, this episode stands out as one of the most graphic responses to calling that I've ever seen. This duck had been several hundred yards away and totally oblivious of our presence. But then he probably heard just one or two notes from the call, a faint, plaintive beckoning in the distance, and he couldn't get to us fast enough.

Truly, duck calling is a fine art. It is also an acquired skill. Being a good duck caller requires a combination of musical talent and learned hunting lore. Also, being in the right spot goes a long way toward successful calling. A novice caller in a honey hole can land ducks on his gun barrel, while an expert caller in a spot the ducks don't like will likely go home empty-handed. Still, all things being equal, a hunter who has mastered his instrument, who knows ducks' language, and who knows *when* to call as well as *how* to call will fare much better than his counterparts who don't.

First, the talent. Blowing a duck call is like playing a musical instrument. Any decent call can produce an adequate range of notes, and good callers can hit and hold these notes as desired. However, just as some musicians are born with more ability than others, some callers have a God-given talent for using a duck call. They have a musical ear and a natural ability to produce whatever sounds they desire.

Conversely, some would-be musicians can't carry a tune in a bucket, and some would-be duck callers can't make good sounds regardless of how hard they try. They just don't have the gift. They might practice enough to be passable callers, but they will never become virtuosos.

Second, the acquired knowledge. Besides being able to "play" a call, a good duck caller must know *which* calls to make and *when* to make them. He must know how to "read" ducks—gauge their levels of interest or excitement—and then match his calling style to their disposition. This is the difference between noisemakers and duck callers. Some contest callers can blow beautiful duck sounds on stage in front of judges, but they come up short in applying this skill in an actual hunting situation.

This knowledge comes mainly from experience and by observing how seasoned *hunting* callers (as opposed to *contest* callers) work ducks. Timing—knowing when to call—is a critical factor. (Knowing when *not* to call is equally critical.) Volume—how loud or how soft to blow—is another key. Cadence, like the beat in a song, may be rapid or slow. Sometimes ducks prefer fast, excited calling. Other times they respond better to a passive, lazier-type of calling. A caller's challenge is finding the right cadence for a given day, then sticking with it.

Really *good* callers can frequently convince ducks to do things they didn't intend to do and work to places they hadn't planned on going. They understand duck behavior and can read their moods and adjust their calling accordingly. They can grab ducks' attention and not let go. Truly, for many experts, rather than the means to an end, calling is an end unto itself. Instead of shooting ducks, the challenge is calling them in. The satisfaction comes in fooling them and working them to the water.

Calls for Dabbling Ducks

Duck calls have been fashioned out of an almost endless range of natural and man-made materials: wood, plastic, rubber, cane, bone, antler, hose pipe, old shotgun shells, etc. Most modern commercial calls are mass-produced in factories. Others are handmade or partially handmade in a craftsman's shop and tuned to their maker's desires. The former are relatively inexpensive, costing $20 to $40 on average. The cost of the latter reflects their uniqueness. Handmade duck calls frequently sell for more than $100.

Most duck hunters use calls that mimic the sounds of a mallard hen, which are effective on several dabbling duck species. However, pintail/widgeon whistles, wood duck "squealers," gadwall calls, mallard drake calls, and other specialty calls are available. These calls offer options for a more natural approach in calling a particular species. Still, to most dabbler hunters, "duck calling" refers to mallard suzy sounds.

Duck calls can be divided into three basic categories: Arkansas-style (a single plastic reed held in place with an integral toning board and cork wedge); Cajun/Louisiana-style (multiple plastic reeds with the reeds, toning board, and wedge all separate and held together by forced pressure when the stopper is inserted into the barrel); and Reelfoot-style (single metal reed with the reed, toning board, and wedge separate and held together by forced pressure when the stopper is inserted into the barrel).

The name of each of these calls defines its origins and hints at its intended use. Arkansas calls are designed primarily for use in flooded timber and also for calling competitions. They produce clean, mellow notes (little rasp), and they are soft to moderate in volume. They are best for hunting situations where ducks are working close. Calls that are too loud may cause unnatural echoing in the woods.

Dabbler hunters carry an assortment of calls for a variety of situations.

Cajun/Louisiana calls are designed to attract ducks across open marsh or flooded agricultural fields. They are raspy, moderately loud, and very realistic-sounding. They are the easiest calls for beginning and medium-skilled callers to use effectively.

Reelfoot calls are best at luring ducks over long distances of open water or from high altitudes. Their metallic, ringing notes are loud, and they have "reach" in windy conditions. These calls require a lot of lung power, which makes them hard for beginners to blow properly.

Hunters should select and use a call that best matches their particular hunting location and situation. In a swamp or timber, an Arkansas call has the right pleading tone. In marsh country and flooded agricultural fields, a Cajun/Louisiana call has the proper combination of volume and natural sound. And for hunting on big open water (lakes, reservoirs, large rivers), a Reelfoot call will be most effective when blown by a caller who is proficient with it.

This isn't to say that any call won't work in any situation when blown by a skilled caller. Success with *any* duck call has a lot to do with personal preference and confidence. If a hunter thinks a call sounds good and he knows how to control its pitch, volume, and cadence he can generally make it work anywhere.

Learning to Call

Many older duck callers learned to call at the knee of their forebears. Such one-on-one instruction was hard to beat, but many modern hunters don't have this luxury. Not to worry. Today's hunters can take advantage of a broad selection of how-to-call cassette tapes, videos, and CDs. Now beginners can learn first-hand from the nation's best callers.

Instructional tapes and videos normally begin with the basics— how to hold a call,

© Bill Buckley

Many hunters practice calling while driving...alone, with the windows up.

how to put air into it (from the diaphragm, not puffed-out cheeks!), how to control volume and cut off notes, etc. Next, they explain "duck talk"—natural calls that mallard hens make, when they make them, and what they mean. Then they teach hunters how to blow such call series as the hail call (highball), come-on call, feed chatter, comeback call, and lonesome hen.

With a good instructional tape, a capable instrument, and some concerted effort, any hunter can become a passable caller. Listen to the basic calls on the tape, then practice imitating them. Do this over and over, paying particular attention to the cadence and how the notes scale down. Try taping your calls, then playing them back and listening with a critical ear. This way you can hear mistakes that you won't notice when actually blowing the call. (One good time to practice calling is when driving your vehicle.)

Beginning callers should work to master the basic hail call (5 to 7 notes in descending pitch), come-on call (similar to the hail call, but faster and with more excitement), feed chuckle (good fill-in call for when ducks are circling close), comeback call (5 to 7 fast descending notes with a drawn-out, pleading urgency on the first note), lonesome hen (4 to 6 descending notes with a drawn-out first note and a slow, contented-sounding cadence on remaining notes), and contented hen quacks (low, spaced-out notes of equal volume). Hunters who learn these six calls can hunt effectively, and they have the building blocks for mastering more-complex calling routines.

One time-honored tip in duck calling still holds: Find live ducks and study and learn to mimic their calls. This can be done at refuges, marinas, city parks, or hunting clubs (before season). Get as close to the ducks as possible, sit quietly, listen to their calls, and observe how the birds relate to one another. When listening, practice imitating their sounds, especially the quiet subtleties that distinguish live duck conversations from those made by most human callers. Learning real ducks' language is equivalent to earning a graduate degree in duck calling.

One other way to learn to call ducks is to spend time in a blind with a guide or an expert hunter and observe his technique. Pay special attention to when he calls as well as how he calls. Ask him to explain his duck calling philosophy—what he thinks works best, and why. Then put this advice to good use.

Different Calling Styles

As explained earlier, different regions gave birth to different styles of duck calls. In the same light, these regions also fostered different styles of calling. Timber calling is different from marsh calling, and from open-water calling. Granted, a duck is a duck, and basic mallard hen sounds can be effective in any setting. Still, timber, marsh, and open-water styles of calling evolved because they were more effective in their particular locations than generic calling. This is why hunters should learn to adapt their calling method to their surroundings.

Timber calling. Timber calling is close up. Since hunters are on the forest floor, they can't see ducks until they're nearby, so there's no need for loud, long-range calls. Instead, callers in flooded timber try to mimic a mallard hen that's on the water, sees ducks flying overhead, and issues a quick, excited greeting call. Call volume is just high enough to be audible but not so high that it "blows the birds out." Arkansas hunters refer to this style of calling as "grunting," which describes the way they force air from their diaphragm into the call.

Two or more callers frequently call together in flooded timber for more persuasiveness on ducks sailing overhead. Two or three hunters making feed calls have a strong attraction on ducks that are working close. (The Arkansas-style feeding call is a rapid succession of single notes—*tick, tick, tick, tick*—instead of the nonstop run of double notes—*ticka, ticka, ticka, ticka*—that are popular in other areas.)

Perhaps the most important call in flooded timber is the comeback, which should be blown louder and more persuasively than other calls. The idea is to keep a lock on ducks' attention as they sail downwind. Don't give them

Timber hunters keep a close eye on ducks flying overhead and adjust their calls accordingly.

a chance to lose interest. Be forceful with the call until you turn them back your way, then scale back down to a more natural calling sequence as the birds sail near.

Marsh calling. Marsh and flooded field-type calling is more realistic both in calls issued and in frequency of issuance.

Mike McLemore, Huntingdon, TN

"Finish Ducks with Contented Quacks"

Rather than use a feed call when ducks are working close, three-time world champion caller Mike McLemore blows a continuous series of short, low quacks to steer ducks into gun range. "This works both in timber and fields," McLemore explains. "When a flight is making its final turn, when the ducks are getting ready to 'do it,' I'll blow a series of lonesome hen quacks to guide them in. It's sort of like being the pied piper. They'll lock onto those quacks and float right to the call."

McLemore emphasizes that these quacks are short instead of drawn out. They are low in pitch and volume, and they have approximately one-half to one second between notes. "I'll blow these calls until it's time to shoot. Ducks will just pick up on them and come right to you. In my opinion, this is a better way to land ducks than using a feed call."

Marsh and open-field ducks can be seen at a distance, so callers should use fairly loud, persuasive hail calls until the ducks turn. These calls should be 5- to 7-note hail calls, with each note descending slightly in pitch from the previous note.

If a flight fails to respond to a standard hail call, try speeding the notes up to impart more urgency. Or switch to a pleading hail call, where the first note is longer and "begs" the ducks to come.

When they break your way, ease up on calling. Refrain from calling as long as ducks are arcing around the decoys with wings set. But if their wingbeats get erratic, or if they turn to leave the "traffic pattern," issue a quick, excited comeback call to recapture their attention.

The goal is to get the ducks 60 to 70 yards downwind, then to issue a pleading comeback. More times than not the ducks will respond immediately, curling back upwind and descending toward the decoys.

Again, marsh-type calling is centered on natural sounds and calling only as necessary. You get ducks' attention, steer them your direction, then call only when you have to coax them in.

Marsh calling emphasizes natural calls and calling only as necessary.

Open-water calling. In contrast, open-water calling is the least natural of the three main calling styles. It is also the most difficult to blow, requiring much more lung power than timber or marsh calling styles. Open-water calling is intended to attract ducks across long distances. This style is therefore centered on loud volume and high pitch to capture ducks' attention and guide them to the decoys.

Open-water calling is characterized by long highballs that are blown in rapid succession until ducks are "broken down" and working. A caller starts his routine with an extended "attention-getter note," followed by up to 20 shorter notes of the same pitch and volume *(taaaa, ta, ta, ta, ta, ta, ta, ta...)*. When he runs out of air, the caller takes a quick, deep breath and starts again.

He repeats this long highball over and over until the ducks either break formation and head his way or fly out of hearing range.

If the ducks start working, the caller scales down in volume as the birds draw closer, but he continues the same cadence. Some open-water callers never change the cadence until time to shoot. They continue "pecking" with short, incessant notes to hold the ducks' attention while they circle. Others callers intersperse feed calls and single quacks with the runs of short notes for more realism.

The purpose of the open-water style of calling is to compel ducks to listen, to overpower their intent to go elsewhere, and to literally force them to come check out the source of the calling. This style of calling excites ducks. It is much more persuasive than timber or marsh calling, which are more passive and natural-sounding. Indeed, this style of open-water calling is very *unnatural*. There is little resemblance to natural calls that live ducks make.

Open-water calling stresses volume, and is the least natural of the three main calling methods.

Instead, ducks at long range probably hear only a couple of notes of a highball series, or they're captivated by the rapid-fire cadence of notes. Man will never know why this style of calling works on ducks. Instead, callers who are good at it only know that it *will* work, and sometimes it will draw ducks from unbelievably long distances.

A typical scenario is to blow 2 to 3 extended highballs at a passing flight with no effect, then a single duck will angle out of the flight and start bending toward the calling. This is time to "pour it on" to keep this bird from rejoining the flight. If the caller can hold this duck's attention and continue pulling it toward the call, chances are the whole flock will break and follow this leader to the decoys.

Duck Calling Strategy

Being an effective duck caller is a progression. Step number one is obtaining a good call. Step number two is learning to make basic calls. Step number three is expanding on these basic calls and putting them to good use in a hunting situation.

Again, calling ducks is an imprecise skill. What works one day may not work the next. Ducks' moods (i.e., responsiveness to calling) vary according to changes in weather, setting, hunting pressure, and other factors. The mark of a truly good duck caller is being able to figure out what calling strategy works best on any given day. This ability comes through instinct combined with calling experience. The more a hunter calls ducks and observes their reactions to different calling methods, the better he'll become at picking the right one.

How to Call Dabbling Ducks

Following is a short list of variables in duck calling and guidelines for how to adjust calling strategies to match them.

Call a lot, call a little. "How much should I call?" Every duck hunter who has raised a call to his lips has asked himself this question. Call too much, and you may scare ducks away. Call too little, and you may lose their attention and they will go elsewhere. There can be a fine line between these two extremes. Sometimes it only takes a few seconds of *not calling at a critical time* for working ducks to break away and go elsewhere. The best advice is to call only as much as you have to, based on hunting conditions and how the birds are responding. This may mean calling a little or a lot. Figuring out how much to call involves experimenting on a daily basis.

Weather has a big influence on how much to call. Dabbling ducks are more responsive to calling on clear, cold, windy days. Such days typically follow a frontal passage, and new birds may have arrived on the scene. Try calling more—louder, more frequently—when the sky is blue, the temperature is chilly, and the wind is brisk. Conversely, dabbling ducks are usually spookier when the sky is overcast, the temperature warm, and the wind calm. On days like this, calling should be scaled down in volume and frequency.

Hunting location. Setting can play a major role in determining best calling strategy. If ducks are naturally working your spot—if you're where they want to be—calling should be kept to a minimum. A little calling, especially feed calls or a 4- to 5-

note lonesome hen call, might reassure them, but why risk over-calling when the birds are coming anyway? A duck call is both an attractor and a convincer. When ducks are already attracted and convinced, there's little need for it. I believe that in many settings, far more ducks are scared away by overcalling than are lost by undercalling.

However, there are situations when more aggressive calling is required. When ducks are a long way off, or when you're com-

Multiple callers can prove extra persuasive in luring wary ducks.

peting against other callers, you've got to be the most per-suasive caller. In such cases, there's no virtue in being timid. It's like the loudest kid in the class getting the atten-tion. You must get the ducks' attention then keep it as you pull them in.

This is where call volume and pitch are important. Louder, higher-pitched calls are more audible—hence notice-able—from a distance. Duck hunting lore has it that when ducks are being called by multiple callers, everything else being equal, they are more likely to respond to the one blowing the loud-est, highest-pitched call.

One caller, multiple callers. One thing I truly enjoy is lis-tening to and watching two or more veteran callers work a flight

How to Call Dabbling Ducks

Tom Wiley, Starkville, MS

"Use Contented Feel Call Instead of Rolling Chuckle"

for more natural-sounding feed calls, use a sporadic mix of single notes instead of a rolling chuckle, advises Tom Wiley, originator of the Flex Tone duck call. Wiley says, "Ducks make that rolling, continuous chuckle when they're flying, and I've also heard them make it on the water when they're nervous. But their true contented feed call is more a series of single-note sounds that are strung together in a broken rhythm. For instance, I say the word *cut* into my call, and I may say it twice, then once, then three times, then twice again: *cut-cut...cut...cut-cut-cut...cut-cut.* I'll also add in an occasional soft quack or two for more realism. The idea is to not follow a specific rhythm, and use that single-note sound instead of *cuta-cuta-cuta-cuta.*"

of mallards together. This is like listening to an orchestra instead of a soloist. Multiple callers who know how to work together can truly make beautiful music.

Multiple calling is more applicable in situations when ducks need more persuading: open water, gusty winds, competing with other blinds and callers. Conversely, in closer-in or private settings where ducks are eager to come, the extra persuasion of multiple callers isn't usually necessary.

When two or more callers are calling together, one should take the lead and others should take supporting roles. When "maximum persuasion" is needed to gain ducks' attention and turn them, everybody should highball. Make a ruckus! Then,

Chapter Three

"Use a Pintail Whistle on Call-Shy Ducks"

When mallards show signs of being call-shy, try using a pintail whistle instead of a mallard hen call when ducks are working close. Veteran call maker Eli Haydel uses this strategy in the marsh country of southwest Louisiana. He believes it puts ducks at ease and coaxes them in when standard calling methods might scare them away.

"By the time ducks migrate down to where I hunt, they've heard just about every type of call and calling method there is, and they can be extremely leery of regular mallard-type calling," Haydel notes. "When I see evidence of this, I switch off to using the pintail whistle on circling ducks. I always have some pintail decoys in my spread, so the whistle isn't out of place. I blow it so it sounds like two or three pintails whistling at the same time.

"Now, mallards are sociable ducks. They like to land with other species. Also, pintails are very wary ducks, and mallards may recognize this and feel safe landing with pintails. I don't know. All I know is that this trick does the job on days when regular mallard calling won't work."

when the flight has responded and is approaching, everybody but the lead caller should slack off, allowing the lead to be the sole focus of the birds' attention. Other callers might only add feed calls or soft quacks for extra realism. But if the ducks circle a time or two and then appear to be leaving, it's time for other callers to chime back in with excited comeback calls. Make a din of noise that demands that the ducks swing back for another look. Sometimes the flight may continue on their way, but a single or pair might break away and come in.

Once again, there's a fine line between calling too much and calling too little. Multiple calling is more effective on those clear, brisk days when ducks are working better. On still, overcast days when ducks are spooky, multiple calling may hurt more than it helps. Try different approaches to see which is most effective.

One more slant on multiple calling is to have one lead caller actually work the ducks while several other callers simultaneously blow feed chuckles and/or mallard drake calls *(gweep, gweep, gweep)* for additional realism. Anybody can use a shaker-type call that makes a feed chuckle. Several of these calls going together, backing up the best caller who is blowing a standard routine, makes for a powerful attraction to circling ducks. (This is a good way for young or novice hunters to participate in calling.)

Using species-specific calls. As mentioned earlier, most duck calling is "mallard style," but calls are available for other species. Pintail and wigeon whistles, wood duck squealers, teal calls, and gadwall calls (similar to mallard, but softer) are options for calling these birds. Such calls are typically used when these species predominate. For

The pintail whistle is one of several species-specific calls.

instance, when hunters are targeting pintails in Louisiana rice fields (when they have a pintail decoy spread out), blowing pintail whistles will sound more natural and probably be more effective than blowing mallard calls. The same is true for swamp hunters blowing wood duck calls, and for early-season hunters using teal and gadwall calls when these ducks are predominant. Using a species-specific call is simply a refinement in calling strategy. While mallard-style calling might be considered a "shotgun approach" (calls anything), using a species-specific call would be a "rifle approach" aimed to be more effective on that one type of duck. Once again, the only way to find out is to try it.

How to "Read" Ducks

Learning to "read" ducks is one of the highest levels of achievement in duck calling. "Reading" ducks means observing them and being able to judge whether or not they will respond to calling. Expert hunters will ignore some passing flights (not call to them), then call enthusiastically to other flights. The difference is that the latter birds had the right "look." Their location, direction of flight, altitude, speed, and formation provide clues as to whether or not they might work. Sometimes these clues are very subtle, but some callers with years of experience at observing ducks on the wing can decipher them. I've hunted with guides who would watch flight after flight go by without calling, then a flight would come by that was slightly out of the norm. "Those ducks will work," these guides would say, and they'd set about calling the birds with determined enthusiasm. In many cases the ducks *would* work.

"Reading ducks" also involves deciding when to call working ducks based on how they are working. Calling at the right time is as important as making good sounds. Once ducks are locked into a working pattern, the best advice is to go easy with the call, reassuring them from time to time with feed calls and quacks but not trying to overwhelm them. But if the ducks start showing signs of indecision, if they get higher or look like they're about to break out of their working pattern, then it's time to get persuasive. By issuing an excited comeback call, you can sometimes make those ducks lock their wings and cut sharply back to the decoys.

How do you learn to read ducks? You learn through experience and trial and error. You learn through careful observation of how ducks respond to calling. You learn through trying different things. Reading ducks can't be taught by an instructional cassette or CD. It must be learned in the marsh and field and flooded timber.

Indeed, the art of calling ducks is extremely subjective. There are few absolutes except this one: The more you do it, the better caller you'll become. Truly good duck callers are "rare birds" in their own right. There are many more "duck call blowers" than "duck callers." Still, with enough practice and experience, a hunter can progress to this second category. He can develop the right feel and confidence in his calling to actually be able to control what ducks do—at least some of the time.

Working a flight of ducks with a call is one of the supreme accomplishments and pleasures in this sport. Being able to capture ducks' attention, turn them from their original flight path, then convince them to land in your decoys is an achievement. Being able to do this time after time is the true measure of an expert caller.

Chapter Four

Decoys and Decoy Spreads

My decoy bag weighed a ton. It was slung across my back like a giant knapsack, and the dozen-and-a-half magnums bogged me down with each step in the muddy field. I was sweating profusely. I had to stop and catch my breath every 50 or so yards before slogging on toward my goal—a freshly flooded slough where mallards were working like bees around a hive.

I'd found these birds while freelancing on a local river after a heavy rain. I knew the landowner—no problem with permission. All I had to do was tote my decoys, gun, and shell bag from my boat across the plowed field to the honey hole, but I sunk ankle-deep into the mire with each stride. Looking back, why hadn't I lightened the load to a dozen decoys instead of 18? Or even better, it would have been a godsend to have had some foam decoys for such a situation. They would have been like carrying air, while these magnums felt like bowling balls.

© Bill Buckley

Too many decoys can be the straw that breaks the freelancer's back.

Decoys are an integral part of most hunts for dabbling ducks. Only pass-shooters, jump-shooters, and float-hunters don't depend on decoys to lure ducks into gun range. All other styles of hunting are designed around the skillful use of decoys to attract birds' attention (along with calling) and to convince them to join the party.

This is why hunters should learn how to use decoys in a broad range of settings. They must be able to rig for shallow potholes and deep open lakes; set a permanent spread around a fixed blind; deploy small, temporary spreads when freelancing; and impart realism and attraction to decoys on days when the wind is calm and the sky is gray.

Following are guidelines for selecting, rigging, and deploying decoys for a range of situations that hunters may face during their pursuit of ducks. Remember, he who uses decoys best shoots most. This is why hunters should pay more than cursory attention to this most important element of wildfowling.

Decoy Types, Sizes, Species

Duck decoys come in a broad array of materials, sizes, species, etc. Some decoys are better suited than others for particular hunting situations. Here's what's available in decoys, and the settings and uses for which they're most appropriate.

Materials. Most decoys sold today are molded from thermoplastic resins. These decoys are hollow (thus lightweight), extremely lifelike, and moderately tough. Overall, they are great for general use. They also offer extremely good value in terms of cost versus service.

Molded plastic decoys come in both weighted keel and water keel models. Weighted (sealed) keel decoys are self-righting when tossed onto the water, while water keel decoys must be set upright by hand. Weighted keel decoys are slightly heavier and more expensive than water keel decoys. However, weighted keel decoys are far and away the most popular choice among hunters because of their versatility and ease in setting out and picking up. In contrast, water keel decoys are

A drake pintail lights into a spread containing pintail decoys.

more trouble to set out and pick up, and are best-suited for permanent spreads (set out and left for extended periods).

The main drawback to hollow plastic decoys is their vulnerability to stray shot. Water will leak into the body through just one pellet hole, causing the decoy to partially submerge or sink.

Hard foam decoys are an option to hollow plastic decoys, and they are unsinkable. These decoys are made by pouring foam beads into molds, then applying heat to expand them to fill the molds. These solid body decoys are extremely durable, and they ride well in rough water. Their drawbacks are their weight—approximately double that of hollow plastic decoys—and their cost, which is some 50 percent more than equivalent hollow plastic decoys. Hard foam decoys are favorites among hunters who shoot over permanent spreads on open water.

Soft foam shell decoys are a blessing to hunters who hike into hard-to-reach marshes, beaver ponds, etc. These decoys weigh next to nothing. They also "swim" realistically in the lightest breeze. Their drawbacks are their

Carry-Lite water keel decoys.

less realistic appearance and the greater time and effort required to set them out. Heads must be inserted into shell bodies, and soft foam decoys must be set on the water by hand—not just tossed out. Also, sometimes these decoys will flip over in gusty winds.

Rubber, cork, and wooden decoys are available to hunters, but these represent a very small percentage of the market, and they offer few advantages over decoys made from more common materials.

Decoys and Decoy Spreads

Sizes. Factory decoys are manufactured in three sizes— standard, magnum, and super magnum. Standard decoys are about the same size as live ducks (approximately 16 inches). Magnums measure approximately 18 inches, while super magnums stretch to approximately 22 inches. Correspondingly, a dozen standard hollow plastic decoys (not including anchors) weighs approximately 11 pounds, while magnums and super magnums weigh 15 and 30 pounds respectively.

Why the different sizes? The answer has to do with visibility. It's easier for passing ducks to see bigger decoys than smaller ones. Magnum and super magnum decoys have more "presence," hence attraction, than standards.

Still, standard decoys are more than adequate in many hunting situations, especially where ducks are working close—i.e., in small marshes, flooded timber, etc. Magnums and super magnums are preferable on big marshes, open lakes, and rivers where ducks can see farther.

Also, standard decoys are the choice of many freelance hunters because of their smaller size and weight. As the illustration in this chapter's introduction points out, decoys that are too big and heavy can be burdensome to hunters who must walk or wade to where ducks are working.

Species. Duck decoys are available in several species. Far and away, the predominant decoy species used by North American duck hunters is the mallard. Mallard decoys have an attraction to all dabbling ducks. Hunters going after a mixed bag can set out only mallard decoys with confidence that they will lure other dabbler species as well.

Most hunters use a number of mallard decoys in their dabbler spreads.

However, decoys are available in virtually all dabbler and diver species. Many hunters set spreads consisting predominantly of mallards but including a scattering of other species for additional visibility and realism. For instance, the white color on pintail drakes is visible—and eye-catching—over long distance, so it's a good idea to mix a few pintails into a mallard spread, especially where these two species share the same area.

Another example: Black duck decoys mixed in with mallards will increase a spread's visibility over long distance. Some savvy hunters rig with black duck decoys comprising half (or more) of their mallard spread to make it show up better. (See sidebar on page 108.)

Variety is often the spice that brings a decoy spread to life in the eyes of passing ducks.

Adding teal, wigeon, gadwall, spoonbill, and other decoys to a mallard spread imparts a more natural look. Whether this attracts more ducks is questionable, but doing so certainly won't diminish a spread's effectiveness. Also, many open-water hunters set out both dabbling and diving duck decoys where both types of birds coexist.

Hunters who target a particular species other than mallards frequently tailor their spreads accordingly. Examples are pintail hunters in areas where these ducks predominate. A spread of mostly pintail decoys will draw these birds better than mallard decoys. Still, the latter decoys will work in cases where such specialization isn't practical.

Adding a white decoy like this bufflehead drake can increase a spread's visibility.

Special-Effect Decoys.

Many special-effect decoys are available to duck hunters. These include feeders (duck butts), sleeper decoys, and confidence decoys (herons, gulls, crows, coots). All these are meant to impart greater realism to a spread, to keep it from looking "static." They are designed to communicate to working ducks that food is available or that birds on the water are safe and content.

How much these special-effect decoys add to a spread's effectiveness is a matter of debate. Any benefits would more likely come in a smaller spread, where individual decoys would be more noticeable. Benefits would be less noticeable in a large decoy spread.

Sleeper Decoy.

Feeder Decoys.

Larry Smittle, Checotah, OK

"Use Confidence Decoys to Attract More Ducks"

Using confidence decoys will help duck hunters draw more birds into range, attests veteran hunter Larry Smittle. Confidence decoys are non-duck decoys that lend an air of realism and comfort to ducks trying to decide whether or not to land in a spread.

"Coot decoys are good early-season confidence decoys," Smittle notes. "Dabbler ducks are used to sharing water with coots. Also, coots pull up and scatter aquatic vegetation, making it available for shallow-diving ducks to share. Pintails, wigeon, gadwall, and other ducks know they can get a good meal where coots are feeding. So when coots are in the area where I'm hunting, I'll always set at least a dozen coot decoys out to the side of my duck decoys."

Later in the season, when the coots have gone, Smittle sets out 6 to 12 Canada goose decoys, both for greater visibility and confidence. These also go on the outside edge of his duck decoys, typically on the upwind side.

"One more thing I do is set a great blue heron decoy or a couple of crow decoys around the edge of my duck decoys," Smittle continues. "I really think they add to a spread's realism. I believe ducks know that blue herons and crows are wary birds, and if there were any threat they wouldn't be hanging around. So seeing them makes ducks feel secure and more believing that the duck decoys on the water are real."

Decoys and Decoy Spreads

Standup, Stake-Out Decoys

Two other types of decoys are standups and stake-outs, and their names describe how they are used. Standups are full-body decoys molded to look like ducks standing and/or feeding on dry land. These decoys come with broad-base stands to keep them from tilting over. However, they will still blow over in a stiff wind. They should be anchored through the base with stakes or pieces of stiff wire to hold them in gusty breezes.

Stake-outs are half-body shell decoys that come with removable heads and stakes for setting up in mud, sand, etc.

Both of these types of decoys are designed for use on dry land or in very shallow water. They look more realistic than floating decoys in these settings.

Stake-out decoys placed in shallow water or on dry land will look like standing/feeding ducks.

Number of Decoys

How many decoys are enough? This depends on each hunting situation. Two might be plenty on a beaver pond where ducks are used to working. On the other hand, 200 or 2,000 (I've actually seen a spread with this many decoys!) might be deployed to lure in dabbling ducks on big open water.

Generally, a bigger spread has more attraction ("pulling power") to passing ducks than a smaller spread. Ducks like a lot of company, and sometimes they will divert from their intended destination to land with a large decoy spread under their flight path. On the other hand, they will also readily work to a small-er number of decoys set where they intended to go to start with.

To a great extent, decoy numbers are determined by a hunter's hunting tactics and capabil-ities. If he's a free-lancer walking into

The number of decoys you use, and their placement, will depend on the hunting situation.

a pond, marsh, or flooded timber, it's a chore carrying more than a dozen decoys in a shoulder bag over a long distance. Boat hunters can transport more; 3 to 6 dozen are a good average. And hunters who hunt from permanent blinds and who leave their decoys out for extended periods can deploy hundreds of decoys.

Again, how many decoys are enough? As many as the situation calls for. As many as a hunter can afford. As many as he can transport and set out and pick up. With decoys it's hard to have too many, but it's easy to *try to handle* too many.

How to Rig Decoys

"Rigging" means attaching line and an anchor to a decoy so it will stay in place when set on the water. Most decoys for dabbling ducks are rigged "straight line" style: a length of line tied to the decoy's keel with a weight attached at the other end.

Various types of line are used to rig decoys, but some are better than others. Nylon line is the choice of many hunters. Nylon line is strong, rot-proof, and it sinks and holds knots well. Nylon line comes in such colors as drab olive and brown (far better than white), and it is relatively inexpensive.

Nylon line is available in two varieties—twisted and braided. Twisted line has 3 strands that are twisted together. Braided line has 8 or 12 strands that are braided together, and this braid provides much more strength and abrasion-resistance. However, braided line is considerably more expensive than twisted line.

Braided nylon line.

One popular option is twisted nylon line that is covered in a tar coating. This line has a stiffness, knot-holding ability, and dark brown color that make it especially suitable for rigging decoys. (One special note for rigging with nylon line: Always melt line ends with a match to keep strands from unraveling.)

Another rigging option is PVC-extruded line, a rubbery green line that is tangle resistant. This line is sold under several brand names (Tanglefree, Avery Knot-Proof, H.S. Quick-Rig Decoy Cord). It is strong and rot-proof. It doesn't hold knots well, so line crimps or anchors with built-in crimps are recommended. (Crimps are small metal or plastic locking devices through which line is routed and doubled back, then mashed tight to keep the line from slipping.)

Decoy anchors can be anything that will sink and hold a decoy in place. These may be railroad spikes, tire weights, large bolts, spark plugs, etc. However, through the years innovative waterfowlers have devised a variety of molded lead anchors specifically for decoys, and these generally perform better than "make-do" anchors listed above.

The strap anchor is perhaps the most widely used. The strap anchor is a long, thin lead bar with a hole in one end. This design allows hunters to wrap the weight around a decoy's neck to hold the line in place during transport and storage. This type of weight is very convenient for hunters who move about frequently. It is best for shallow, soft bottoms where currents and wind aren't excessive.

Strap anchor

Mushroom and pyramid anchors are better suited for open water, where strong currents and winds may be encountered. These anchors are designed to dig into the bottom and hold when pulled sideways.

Two good knots for rigging decoys with nylon line are the slip knot and the improved clinch knot. Before tying a slip knot, tie a simple overhand knot in the end of the line to serve as a stop when the slip knot is cinched down.

Some hunters rig with swivels, clips, or snaps to prevent line twist and to facilitate the quick connection of lines to decoys. Such hardware is especially applicable for deep, rough water. However, for most hunters and hunting situations, a simple straight-line rig—line tied directly to decoy keel and anchor—is adequate.

Mushroom anchor

How long should decoy lines be? Freelance hunters should rig with lines that are 6 feet. This length will work in water from a few inches to over 5 feet deep, which covers most dabbler hunting situations. This length

Pyramid anchor

allows some flexibility when moving around to hunt different spots. Obviously, hunters who know the water depth will be much shallower or deeper where they will be hunting can adjust their anchor lines accordingly.

Hunters who set out permanent spreads should rig for little slack to keep decoys from tangling. A good rule of thumb is to measure water depth, then add two more feet to anchor lines so decoys can swim and to accommodate for slight rises in water elevation. Then decoys should be set at least 2 feet apart. This system will avoid tangles when the wind shifts and decoys swing about.

Simple Decoy Sets for Dabbling Ducks

How should hunters deploy decoys to lure in dabbling ducks? Which sets work best in different situations? Are random sets better, or should hunters adhere to time-honored designs that use Js, Vs, and fishhooks?

Chapter Four

"In a Competitive Setting, Use More Super Magnum Black Duck Decoys"

❝When I'm hunting in a crowd, I want my decoy spread to be more obvious than my competitors', to stick out more," says Hunter McLemore, who hunts virtually every day of the season in west Tennessee. "To achieve this, I use approximately 75 percent black duck decoys, and I also like super magnum decoys. This combination provides a big, very obvious image that's a lot more visible than a spread consisting of regular mallard decoys. This is especially true on sunny days. Those big black decoys really stand out."

McLemore got this idea while observing ducks at a local refuge. "The black ducks show up a lot better than other ducks. Also, unless you're really close to ducks on the water, it's hard to distinguish colors. Usually you just see black silhouettes."

McLemore says he's had extremely good success with this spread. "It's much better at pulling ducks than a regular spread. Also, I've never seen any indication whatever that ducks are suspicious of it in spite of all the dark-colored oversized decoys."

Dabbling ducks are hunted in a broad range of settings, from beaver ponds to big lakes to dry fields. Each setting and situation has its own requirements for decoy effectiveness. Generally, little ponds and potholes call for a smaller number of decoys dispersed erratically to simulate live ducks in a casual, secure disposition. On the other hand, big water requires larger, more visual spreads set in precise patterns to lure ducks into predetermined kill zones.

Certainly, setting decoys is an imprecise science, and *where* decoys are set is infinitely more important than *how* they are set.

Decoys tossed out with no aforethought on a hole where ducks are used to working may still be eminently effective.

Still, hunters should understand and use a few basic rules in setting out decoys that will make their spreads look more natural—hence convincing—and which will help them funnel ducks where they want them. Following are basic sets and advice for the most common situations that dabbler duck hunters face.

Pothole/marsh portable spread. Eighteen to 36 decoys are usually plenty in this close-in setting, and they should be mostly mallards with a few pintails and black ducks added in (if black ducks are natural in the area). Set individual clusters of 3 to 6 decoys on the upwind and crosswind sides of the pothole. The overall shape may be a U, but the clusters don't run together to form long strings. The idea is to simulate small family groups of ducks that are secure and content.

Pothole/marsh portable spread

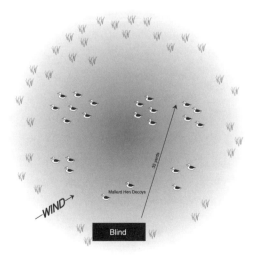

Pothole/marsh permanent spread. Again, more decoys generally have more pulling power, so some fixed-blind hunters set permanent spreads that are several times the size of portable spreads. Many permanent spreads number more than 100 decoys, and 200 aren't uncommon on large ponds. Most of these spreads are arranged in some form of a U or V, with the open end of the spread facing the prevailing downwind direction and the blind situated at the head of the spread. Thus the blind is facing open water, and "arms" of decoys angle off each corner. Average length of these "arms" would be 35 yards. One secret to this spread is to make sure the landing hole is large and distinct enough to attract ducks regardless of wind direction.

Pothole/marsh permanent spread

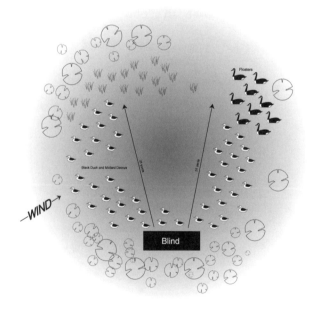

Open-water permanent spread. Many decoy sets are used for dabbling ducks on open water, but one tried-and-true design is the "two-set rig" which uses two distinct groups of decoys with an open landing zone in the middle. Simply divide decoys into two equal groups. Set one group out from one corner of the blind, extending no farther than 45 yards from the front edge of the blind. Then set the second group off the other corner of the blind at an equal distance to the first group. Leave a large, open landing zone directly in front of the blind, between the two decoy groups.

Open-water permanent spread

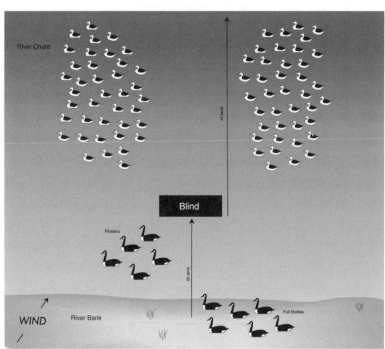

Chapter Four

Flooded timber spread. Most hunting in flooded timber is done around "holes," which are openings in the forest canopy through which ducks can work down to the water. Decoys should be arranged around the sides and upwind edge of a hole, leaving the middle open for ducks to land. Also, scatter several decoys into the woods a few yards back from the opening. The idea is to simulate a flock of ducks that has landed and is now swimming into the timber to feed and loaf. A dozen to 60 decoys is plenty for hunting in flooded timber, depending on the size of the hole and the number of hunters available to tote decoys.

Flooded timber spread

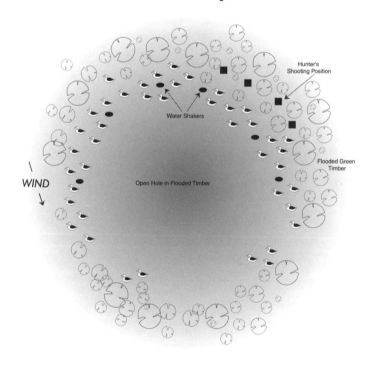

Hunter's Shooting Position

Water Shakers

Flooded Green Timber

WIND

Open Hole in Flooded Timber

Tommy Akin, Greenfield, TN

"Muddy Water in Decoys Simulates Feeding Activity"

Tommy Akin has hunted ducks more than 40 years in west Tennessee's flooded timber and fields. Akin and his lease partners know from experience that muddy water in and around their decoys is attractive to ducks overhead. He says, "When real ducks feed in a corn or soybean field, they stir up mud off the bottom when they're grubbing around after grain. The effect is like a muddy cloud in the water.

"We simulate this by driving a four-wheeler through our decoys to kick up mud. (Akin's spread floats in only 12 inches of water.) We do this every morning before we start hunting, and we'll do it again a couple of hours later if the mud starts settling out.

"Ducks are greedy birds, and when they see what they think is feeding going on, sometimes they can't wait to drop in to get their share. We've experimented with this enough to know that having that muddy water really makes a difference, especially on high-flying birds that can look down and see the mud before they can see the decoys."

Lakeshore/island point spread. If wind or currents aren't too strong, dabbling ducks like to loaf around a shoreline or island point that juts out into a lake, reservoir, or river. In this situation, a larger, more visible spread is advisable since ducks may be passing at longer distances. Five to 6 dozen magnum or super magnum duck decoys (including a few pintails for greater visibility) and several Canada goose floaters are recommended. In a crosswind, set the duck decoys in a fishhook or checkmark pattern with the long arm running downwind approximately 45 to 50 yards. This arm should be thin toward the end, then thickened as it approaches the blind. Finally, this arm is curled back, leaving an open pocket in front of the blind. (Another description of this spread is a "curving teardrop," with the point of the teardrop downwind.) Canada goose floaters should be clustered together at the upwind head of the spread. Ducks will swing downwind of the decoys, then they'll hook back and follow the long arm up to the main concentration and land in the pocket.

In this same setting, when the wind is blowing from the back of the blind, arrange the decoys in two separate arms to form a wide V with the blind in the point of the V.

Lakeshore/island point V spread

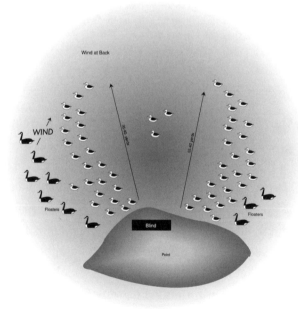

Dry field spread

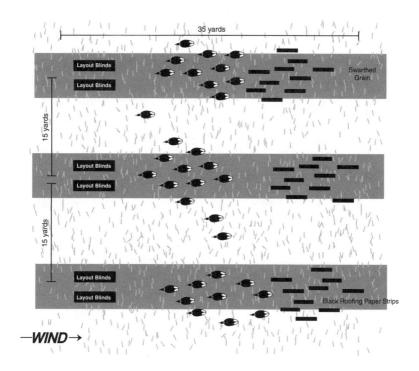

Dry field spread. As explained in chapter 2, "spotting" is the first step to success in hunting field-feeding ducks. Scouters must determine the *exact* spot where ducks are feeding, then set their decoys there for the next early morning or late afternoon feeding cycle. One hundred yards away may miss the mark.

Dig pits or arrange layout blinds in a row facing downwind, then spread decoys to the sides and downwind from this position. A U- or gull-wing-shaped spread is effective. Pits or blinds are at the base of the U, and the arms flare out downwind.

Chapter Four

One especially effective decoy set for field-feeding ducks uses a combination of Canada goose decoys and pieces of light-weight black roofing paper. If the crop is swathed, orient this spread along the rows of grain. If there are no swathed rows, arrange decoys in a random downwind streak.

Start with 5 to 6 dozen Canada goose shells, arranged around the shooters and stretching 20 yards downwind. Then scatter duck-sized rectangles of roofing paper downwind of the geese for another 15 yards. The more squares, the better. (Five hundred to 1,000 squares are typical for a 6-man layout spread.) The idea is to make the ground black. These roofing paper squares can be dealt like playing cards with little regard as to how they land. They simply provide ducks with mass and color in an otherwise featureless field. The goose decoys provide enough realism to keep ducks from spooking. When conditions are prime (blustery, overcast), this spread is deadly.

Adding Movement to Decoy Spreads

To lure ducks in, decoys must appear realistic. To appear realistic, decoys must move. Real ducks move around almost constantly on the water, feeding, preening, drakes chasing hens, etc. If working ducks check out a decoy spread and see no movement or agitated water, they get suspicious in a hurry.

This problem is more worrisome when winds are calm. When winds are blowing, decoys move about and provide plenty realism. Also, circling ducks buffeted by gusty conditions don't get to inspect a spread closely. But when winds are light to nil, decoys don't swim on their own, and ducks get a good

This flapper decoy adds realistic movement to a spread.

look. This combination spells rejection of the spread and defeat for hunters.

There are many methods for imparting movement to decoys. Jerk strings have added "life" to decoy spreads for years. Pull a string—make the decoys swim and tip up. A variation of this is the tipper, which simulates a duck tipping up in the water to feed. (Again, pull the string...) Also, mechanical decoys are popular. Check out a waterfowl accessories catalog, and you will find swimmers, tippers, shakers, flappers, wobblers, and more.

And then there are wing-spinner decoys. These roto/moto ducks have been the rage in recent seasons, and for a simple reason. They work. The flash from their spinning wings has attracted ducks with phenomenal success—in fact, so much so that they've created controversy over whether or not they are *too* effective. At this writing, some states have banned wing-spinners, and others are taking a close look at doing so. In the meantime, many hunters believe ducks are getting used to—and wary of—these mechanical decoys, which have appeared in tens of thousands of spreads in all four flyways.

Whether they use jerk strings, tippers, wobblers, wing-spinners, or whatever, hunters should make some provision to impart movement to their decoy spreads. Especially when hunting conditions are less than favorable and ducks need more convincing, movement can spell the difference between success and failure. Following are specifics on how these various movement options can be employed.

Jerk string. A jerk string consists of a line running from the blind through the decoys and secured to an anchor or stationary

object on the far side of the spread. Incorporated somewhere along the line is a bungee cord, a length of innertube rubber or some other stretchy material to give the string an elastic effect. Pull on the

Never pull on the jerk string when the ducks are directly overhead.

string and it stretches. Release it, and it contracts back to its original length. Then one or more decoys are tied onto the string. When the string is pulled, the decoys "swim" toward the blind. When it is released, the decoys reverse direction. Or, when the string is repeatedly pulled with short back-and-forth strokes, the decoys wobble and give off ripples.

Jerk strings can be used by both freelance and permanent blind hunters. Freelancers can pre-tie a jerk string, including metal rings along the line for snapping in decoys. Then they can roll this string up and keep it in a backpack or shell bag, ready for deployment. When they've chosen their hunting site, they can unroll the jerk string, tie the end to some on-site object, unroll the line, then snap in a couple of decoys that have been pre-rigged with clips attached directly to their keels. This whole operation takes less than five minutes, then regular decoys should be set around the jerk string so that the whole spread benefits from its movement.

Jerk-string rig

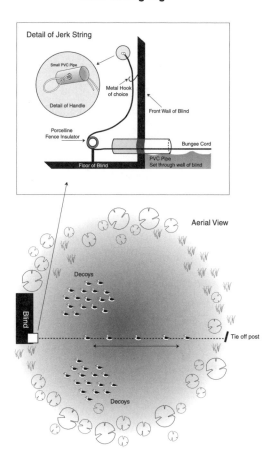

Chapter Four

Fixed-blind hunters who hunt over permanent decoy spreads can get more elaborate with jerk strings. Many hunters rig multiple strings with several decoys attached to each string. These strings run like fingers through the spread. Each hunter has his own string to pull. With several strings working at once, the whole spread comes alive. The effect can be mesmerizing to circling ducks.

Another setup is to run a multi-decoy jerk string down each side of the landing zone. As explained earlier, many permanent spreads consist of a decoy grouping off one corner of the blind and another grouping off the other corner, leaving a hole in the middle. A hunter in each corner of the blind works his own string. This system concentrates decoy movement where circling ducks' attention is focused—on the opening where they will land. This is a highly effective way to convince ducks to come in.

One special consideration with jerk strings is *when* to pull. *Don't* pull when ducks are directly overhead or when they are in close, getting a good look. They might spot a hunter's movement in the blind and flare away. Also, back-and-forth decoy movement isn't realistic in its own right. Instead, the *water agitation* is what looks natural. So pull on jerk strings when ducks *aren't* getting a good look—i.e., after they've passed over the spread, circled downwind, gone behind the blind, etc. Then pull quickly and repeatedly to get as much water agitation as possible. When the ducks come back over, ease up on the strings.

Tipper decoy. A tipper is a variation of a jerk string that involves a single decoy rigged to tip up like a feeding duck when the string is pulled. A tipper is normally used in a confined hole and with a smaller spread. The tipper should be placed in or at the edge of the open landing zone, where it's most noticeable to circling ducks.

Rigging a tipper requires two 5-pound weights (cans of concrete) with screw eyes secured in the top, a length of strong cord, and a decoy. Run the cord from the blind to where the decoy will be set. Pass the cord through the screw eye of the first weight. Next pass the cord through the hole in the decoy's keel where the anchor string would normally be tied. Then tie the end of the line into the screw eye of the second weight. When arranged properly, the two weights are a couple of feet apart on the bottom of the marsh with the decoy floating above and between them. When the string is pulled from the blind, the decoy will tip up and bob like a live feeding duck. This deception has a strong impact on real ducks scrutinizing the spread.

Tipper decoy rig

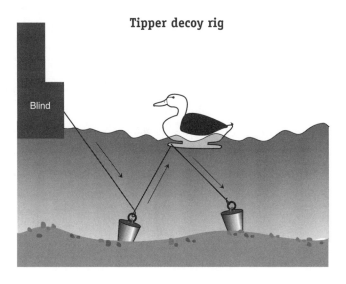

Blind

Chapter Four

Mechanical decoys. Many types and styles of mechanical decoys are available for adding movement to a decoy spread. Some

© Bill Buckley

This feeder decoy quivers to add realistic ripples to the water.

decoys swim. Some wobble. Others flap their wings. Still others pump or splash water in various ways.

Some of these decoys involve bilge pumps or small electric motors with revolving arms, etc. Some larger motion and/or noise makers include elaborate frames to hold multiple decoys and propellers to churn water. Most of these devices are run by electrical power from internal batteries or from 12-volt batteries connected to the decoys through underwater wires.

Each hunter should choose whatever mechanical decoys he desires based on his particular hunting situation, his economics, and his personal preference. Again, any device that adds movement (especially water movement) will increase a decoy spread's realism on days when there is little or no wind.

Wing-spinners. Wing-spinner decoys are what their name implies: decoys with rigid wings that rotate at a high rate of speed. These wings are dark on one side and white on the other. The alternating dark-white flash simulates a duck flapping its wings to land. This motion is easily detectable from a distance, and it has a proven, sometimes almost magical, attraction to ducks.

However, because of their effectiveness, wing-spinner decoys have now sprung up in decoy spreads throughout North America. Many hunters believe ducks are becoming used to seeing them and even grow wary of them. Some hunters are using remote control switches to turn their wing-spinners off once ducks begin working a spread.

Since ducks can't talk, nobody knows for sure if they are, indeed, learning to avoid wing-spinner decoys. Nevertheless, many hunters swear they continue to have greater success by using these decoys than by not using them. In fact, some report very good shooting over spreads that contain multiple wing-spinners—as many as a half dozen.

As mentioned previously, some states have banned wing-spinner decoys, and others are studying their use and considering a ban. But in those states where these decoys are allowed, it's each hunter's decision as to whether or not to use

Wing-spinner decoy.

them. Certainly, they probably work better in areas where hunting pressure is not heavy and they're "the only game in town." These decoys probably lose some of their effectiveness in heavily hunted areas where one or more wing-spinners marks every decoy spread.

Also, experience with wing-spinners bears out that they're more effective in certain types of weather. Best conditions for

Chapter Four

Terry Denmon, Monroe, LA

"Don't Call When Ducks are Coming to a Wing-Spinner Decoy"

Terry Demon is president of Mojo Decoys (Bastrop, LA), which makes and markets the Mojo Mallard wing-spinner decoy. He says, "One big mistake many hunters make is calling to ducks that are locked up and coming to a wing-spinner. As long as they're coming, don't blow the call! There's no reason to add encouragement if the ducks are committed. But if they start to turn away, blow the call to regain their attention. Then, when they're locked and coming again, put the call down and let the wing-spinner decoy do its job."

using them are when it's clear, cold, and blustery—good mallard days. Worst conditions for wing-spinners are when it's overcast, warm, and calm.

A wing-spinner decoy should be set in the decoy spread where the hunter wants ducks to land. Typically, this is in the landing hole 15 to 25 yards in front of the blind. Don't make the mistake of placing this decoy too far away.

Wing-spinner decoys are erected on poles, and height above water makes little difference. Two to 3 feet above the water or ground is plenty.

If multiple wing-spinners are used, group them together (like a flock landing) instead of spreading them out. In this case, staggered heights may be more realistic.

Face wing-spinner decoys into the wind, the way real ducks would land. To do this, tilt the support pole slightly downwind, so that the decoy's butt is lower than its head and its head is pointed into the wind. Then the decoy will act like a weather vane and hold this orientation into the wind.

Decoys and Decoy Spreads

Summary

Use of decoys provides some of the greatest challenges and pleasures in duck hunting. In the off-season, hunters repair, repaint, and rerig decoys for better service and realism. They devise new schemes for decoy spreads that will be more effective than last season. They plot how to gain more movement, how to make their decoys more noticeable, and how to arrange them better.

Then, when the season comes in, many hunters constantly tinker with their spreads, moving decoys, adding and subtracting, trying new ideas. Hunting dabbling ducks is a constant process of trying to outsmart the birds, and decoys are one area that attracts much of this effort.

In 2000, Ducks Unlimited published my book *Decoys and Proven Methods for Using Them*. This volume covers all the subjects mentioned in this chapter, but in much greater detail. It also includes diagrams and explanations of duck and goose decoy spreads used by guides and veteran waterfowlers throughout the U.S. and Canada. Hunters interested in obtaining a copy of *Decoys and Proven Methods for Using Them* can do so directly through the "bookstore" on Ducks Unlimited's Web site at www.ducks.org/bookstore/.

Chapter Five

Duck Blinds

There are duck blinds, and then there are DUCK BLINDS!

I'd seen hundreds of blinds in my 40-plus years of duck hunting, but never anything like the one built by a guide-friend in west Tennessee. A 40-foot metal fuel tank was laid lengthwise and braced up several feet above the water on telephone poles. A plank shooting deck had been constructed along one side. Eighteen hunters could line up and blaze away at incoming birds.

Two doors provided access from the deck into the tank—like walking into a submarine. Inside the tank was a "ready room" with propane heaters, electric lights, comfortable seats, stove, sink, television, and bathroom. If shooting was slow, this guide's clients could stir chili and watch a football game (or snooze) while waiting for birds to show up.

This colossus was positioned on the edge of an oblong hole in green timber. In spite of its enormity, it was totally covered with thick brush. Ducks circling overhead couldn't pick out anything unnatural in the woods below. They loved the spot and would sail in with abandon.

If I were handing out duck hunting Academy Awards, this one would win "Best Blind," but I've seen others that would be close runners-up. Another friend's blind in west Kentucky was dubbed the "Hilton" for its size and comfort. Yet another acquaintance hunted ducks and geese from a pit that was more like a clubhouse buried underground, with theater seats, pool table, and full kitchen with bar.

Some blinds offer many of the comforts of home.

On the other end of the spectrum, I've hunted from muddy holes dug in grainfields; behind screens of cane hastily erected along the edges of river chutes; beneath a white sheet on a snow-covered lakeshore; and in folds of large cypress trees that really weren't blinds at all, but which were highly effective in hiding me from ducks' prying eyes.

The word *blind* is normally an adjective, but in waterfowl hunting it's most certainly a noun. Its definition is *anything that obscures or prevents sight*. In this vein, a duck blind is a structure or device that shields hunters from these wary birds' view. Blinds can be permanent or temporary. They can be fixed or mobile. They can be elaborate, as above, or they can be simple.

Besides concealing hunters, duck blinds also reflect the psyche of their builders. They are expressions of their personality and indicators of their optimism. Blinds reveal their builders' ingenuity and their pride of workmanship. Many blinds are the result of hours of planning and hard work and the expenditure of funds (seemingly) unlimited.

Along with good decoy spreads and calling, having an effective blind is a key to successful duck hunting. Following are considerations for designing, building, positioning, camouflaging, and maintaining various types of blinds for their most effective use possible.

Types of Blinds

"Form follows function" is a famed architectural maxim, and it certainly applies in designing duck blinds. Ducks are hunted in a broad range of settings—open water, marsh, flooded timber, rivers, dry fields. Successful blinds are those that are tailored to specific spots and which satisfy a short list of basic requirements.

For starters, blinds should totally hide hunters, both from the sides and overhead. Again, their main purpose is concealment.

But duck blinds' secondary purpose is also important. When feasible, a blind should offer some degree of comfort and protection from natural elements. Hunters who are shielded from wind, cold, rain, and snow will hunt longer, and this increases their odds of "being there" when the ducks fly.

Chapter Five

Blinds are divided into two categories: permanent and portable. As their name implies, permanent blinds are fixed in place. They are set on spots that ducks regularly frequent, and they remain in place through the season. Hunters go to permanent blinds and wait for the ducks to come to them.

The theory and practice are just opposite with portable blinds. Hunters who use boat blinds or who erect on-the-spot blinds have the luxury of mobility. They can move when the ducks move, setting up in a new spot as often as desired. Portable blinds typically don't have the comforts that many permanent blinds offer, but they make up for any lack of convenience with action and adventure. Nothing makes for a good duck hunt like being in the right spot on the right day. Hunting from a portable blind affords this luxury.

Permanent Blinds

Many permanent blinds are immobile. They are built on dry ground or on stake platforms over water, nailed into trees, dug into the ground, etc. Examples are a stake blind on the edge of a pothole, a blind framed up between trees in flooded timber, or a pit buried in the ground on the edge of a marsh or lake.

Other permanent blinds float on foam logs, pontoons, or barrels. Still others are built on trailers or skids so they can be towed from one spot to another. However, their mass and the inconvenience of moving them separates them from portable blinds. Large floating blinds may be shifted to adjust their location, but they aren't normally repositioned on a daily basis. An example would be a floating blind anchored on a shallow lake flat or on the end of an island in a large river.

What are the advantages of permanent blinds? Their main advantages are comfort and convenience. Again, hunting from a

permanent blind is a waiting game, and waiting is much easier if it's done in a cozy atmosphere. When the skies are empty, passing hours in a heated blind is much more tolerable than standing in water or huddling on the bank in natural cover. Hunters who are comfortable will usually wait longer for ducks to show up. Hunters who are uncomfortable might not stick around long enough to catch the flight. This is how hunting from a permanent blind increases a hunter's odds for success.

Permanent blinds come in virtually all shapes and sizes.

Also, permanent blinds offer the convenience of having everything ready when a hunter arrives at his hunting site. He simply shows up, tosses out his decoys (if they're not already out), then lights his heater and starts a pot of coffee.

Chapter Five

Duck hunters are an imaginative lot, and this is borne out by the variety of permanent duck blinds they build. The basic blind is a rectangular enclosure that is open on one long side for shooting and roofed-over on the opposite long side for protection from the weather. (The roof should be covered with shingles, tin, or tar paper for waterproofness.) This design is known as the "piano box blind" because of its shape. Hunters pass time sitting under the roof, then rise to shoot over the "gunning rail" when ducks arrive.

An endless range of blinds have sprung from this basic design. Some have rooms leading off the shooting deck. Some are large enough to serve as community centers. More elaborate blinds have an array of features to suit their builder's fancy: sofas, wall heaters, card tables, cooking stoves, cabinets, shelves, etc. Such luxury is limited only by their builder's imagination and resources. All permanent blinds, elaborate and simple, should have notches, nails, or rubber gun-barrel grips at each shooting station to keep guns from falling over. Other recommended accessories would include a fire extinguisher, a weather radio, and a urinal pipe.

Floating blinds have three unique advantages over fixed blinds. Floaters can rise or fall with fluctuating water levels. They can be anchored to swing with the wind so that they're always facing downwind, toward incoming ducks. And they can be towed to different locations and removed from the hunting site when the season ends. (Many public lakes and management areas require this.)

Floating blinds may employ any reliable flotation system. Floating dock sections can be bought or built, then a blind can be erected on the platform. A pontoon boat can easily be transformed into a duck blind. (A pontoon boat trailer affords easy transportation and launching.) Many floating blinds have boat sheds added on so a hunter can drive his boat right into the shed, step out into the blind, and commence hunting.

One consideration in building an above-ground or above-water blind is its profile. Many veteran hunters believe a blind with a low profile is less obvious to passing ducks. I believe this is true in some circumstances but not in others. If the blind is situated in tall vegetation (reeds, buck brush, willows, etc.), it will blend in better if it is no higher than surrounding natural cover. But if the blind stands or floats in the open, its height has little bearing on how obvious it is. Another foot or two of head room won't matter to the ducks, but it can make hunting a lot less cramped for the blind's occupants.

Pits are a special category of "permanent blinds." Pits are holes dug into the ground to conceal hunters. Pits are extremely effective if their openings are well camouflaged. Instead of low profile, these blinds are "no profile." Hunters disappear underground, then rise up to shoot when waterfowl descend into range.

As with above-ground blinds, pits can be elaborate, or they can be simple. Many permanent pits are dug with a backhoe, then framed in with wood or concrete. Other pits are molded from fiberglass or welded from sheet metal, then buried. An underground fuel tank can be customized to make a comfortable, efficient pit. A simple pit is a large metal or plastic barrel or culvert buried up to within a couple of inches of its lip.

Chapter Five

Two perennial problems with pits: They have a tendency to leak water and can be pushed out of the ground by water pressure. If a pit is sunk into damp, low ground, and it's not watertight, some type of pump system will be necessary to keep water pumped out. One good system is a standard sump pump (powered by battery) set in a low spot intentionally formed in a back corner of the pit.

Hunters have devised many different systems to keep pits from popping out of wet ground. Heavy weights, cables and stakes, telephone poles used as "dead men," and other designs have been used to anchor pits down. Hunters considering installation of a new pit should locate and consult other hunters who have experience in anchoring pits and follow their advice for doing so.

One prefabricated pit that I highly recommend is made and sold through

Different pits for different places: a shoreline permanent pit (above), and flooded field pit (below).

the Riverfront Hunt Club in Tekamah, Nebraska. This all-fiberglass pit is shipped ready to bury in the ground. It measures 12 feet long by 50 inches wide. It comes with built-in steps, seats, shelves, and roof panels. Options include shooting hole camo covers, padded seat covers, and tie-down anchors for securing the pit in swampy ground or flooded fields. For more information, contact the Riverfront Hunt Club at 402-374-2582.

Camouflaging

After constructing a permanent blind or pit, the next job is camouflaging it so it will completely hide its occupants and blend into its surroundings. This job is critical. Remember, a blind's purpose is to hide its hunters and allay any suspicions of danger in passing birds. If they see something the least bit unnatural, they will fly away. This is especially true of "old ducks" that have been in an area for an extended time and that have been educated by heavy hunting pressure.

This is why blinds must be *thoroughly* covered with vegetation and other camouflage materials. The only open area should be the shooting hole, and even this should be bordered and perhaps divided by thick brush that will shield hunters' faces.

The first step in camouflaging a permanent blind is applying a coat of non-glossy paint (drab olive or marsh brown). Make sure to paint the inside of the blind as well as the outside, or at least the area that might be visible to overhead ducks looking down through the shooting hole.

Next, many hunters apply a layer of camouflage netting. (This step is optional, not mandatory.) Army 3-D artillery netting is best. Look for it at an army surplus store. Adding a camo net provides more "base" for the natural vegetation, which comes next.

Cover the blind with the same type of vegetation that is predominant where the blind will be located, but don't cut it on-site. Instead, cut it elsewhere in order to preserve the site's naturalness.

Use oak brush in flooded timber. (Prune leafy oak branches

off trees before fall's first frost, and the leaves will stay on better. Or use oak brush—post oak, blackjack oak—that holds its leaves after other species have dropped theirs.) Use cornstalks in flooded cornfields, willows in willow chutes, reeds on reedy lakes, etc. Cane, cedars, buck brush, vines, and various marsh grasses are other good camo materials. Just take a quick visual survey of your hunting site, then decide what to use.

Be sure to cover blinds with vegetation that matches the local habitat.

Many hunters totally cover their blinds with vegetation, but when they're finished the blinds look like...brush-covered boxes. Sometimes it's a good idea to mix two or more types of camouflage together in a patchwork pattern. Also, apply brush so it gives the blind a full, rounded appearance—no straight lines. Hang some vegetation at angles away from the blind to eliminate the boxy look.

Vegetation may be applied to a blind by nailing, tying, or wiring, but one of the best ways is covering the blind with woven wire, then stuffing vegetation into the wire panels or attaching it to the wire with cable ties.

Wayne Clark, Crofton KY

"Cover Shooting Hole with Drop-Down Panels"

Wayne Clark says that one good way to totally conceal hunters in a blind is to fit shooting holes with drop-down panels that screen the holes while ducks are working, but which quickly drop out of the way when it's time to shoot. The following system is designed for shooting out the front of the blind only, not back over the roof.

Clark explains, "Construct the blind so that the roof is tall enough to stand under when standing up straight. Then, when camouflaging the blind, extend brush over the front edge of the roof so hunters in the shooting hole have cover over their heads.

"Next cut stiff hog wire panels to match the size of the shooting holes. Use small metal hinges to attach one edge of each panel to the blind rail in front of each shooting hole. You want the panels set so they will pivot in and out freely. Then construct a prop to hold the panel at a 60-degree angle leaning in toward the opening. If done correctly, when propped up the hog-wire panel will reach almost to the brush extending forward from the roof.

"Finally, attach a camo net and small pieces of brush (oak twigs, cane, etc.) to the front of the panels to conceal hunters standing behind them."

Clark says when panels are constructed in this manner and propped up, hunters can stand behind them and be completely hidden from circling ducks' view. The hunters can watch the birds work, then push the panels so they will drop forward when it's time to shoot. Clark adds, "Using these panels makes a hunt a lot more enjoyable. Hunters don't have to crouch in the corner and look at the floor."

Pay special attention to camouflaging the shooting hole, since this is where the greatest chance exists for suspicious

ducks to spot something unnatural (like an excited hunter's shiny face). One good idea is to add two-by-four dividers between shooting stations, then to paint and attach vegetation to these dividers. When ducks are circling overhead, hunters can hide beneath these dividers to avoid being seen.

Another effective way to camouflage a shooting hole is with drop-down panels that stand up in front of hunters and screen them while ducks are working, but which fall out of the way when it's time to shoot. This concealment system works best on blinds with tall roofs and backs, when shooting will only be out the front.

When a blind stays on site all year long, it's a good idea to transplant and cultivate live vegetation around it to help it blend in. A year or two of natural growth can cause a blind to disappear. Use plenty of fertilizer.

A similar camouflaging trick is to add vegetation around a pothole or pond to help a blind blend in. For instance, if a blind is covered in oak brush, "plant" several small "satellite" oak trees around the hole so the blind isn't so obvious. Drive metal fence posts into the bottom as supports, then wire a tree to each post. This will provide a more natural look and keep the blind from standing out.

Steve Fugate, Paducah, KY

"Attach Brush to Permanent Blinds with Cable Ties"

Many hunters nail leafy brush onto their permanent blinds, and this can be a time-consuming, knuckle-skinning chore. However, brushing a blind can be made fast and easy by using plastic cable ties.

Longtime hunter Steve Fugate explains, "You should use heavy-duty black or brown cable ties that are 8 to 12 inches long. You can buy these at any auto parts store for little expense."

Fugate continues, "After building your blind, wrap the sides and roof with woven wire (4-inch panels), and nail the wire securely to the frame at 3-foot intervals. Then use the cable ties to attach brush to the wire. Just hold the brush where you want it on the blind, then cable the brush and the wire together. Cinch the cable down tightly. I normally camouflage with oak brush, and I'll cable a branch at the top and bottom to keep it from shifting.

"Using cable ties, you can put a boatload of brush on a blind two or three times faster than you can by nailing, and it'll never blow off."

Portable Blinds

Portable blinds are the mark of the freelance hunter. As ducks trade around from one feeding or resting area to another, freelancers follow them, and portable blinds allow the hunters to set up virtually anywhere. Portable blinds aren't typically as roomy, comfortable, or weatherproof as permanent blinds, but they make up for their lack of convenience by being available where the action is. Indeed, when freelancing, hunters go to the birds instead of waiting for the birds to come to them. Portable blinds allow them to hide once a hunting site is selected.

The purposes of portable blinds are similar to those of permanent blinds. They must screen hunters from ducks' view, blend into the landscape, provide some protection from the weather, and provide some means of convenience. But again, their main feature is their transportability. These are "special operations" blinds—lightweight, versatile, and ready to move to the action.

Boat Blinds

One major category of portable blinds is boat blinds. A blind on a boat allows a hunter to become a prospector. He can run rivers, lakes, marshes, flooded fields, and flooded timber looking for ducks. Then, when he finds a concentration, he can toss out decoys, erect his portable blind, and get ready to shoot.

Several manufacturers sell portable blinds that can be adapted and bolted onto any metal boat. These blinds are usually collapsible for running, and can be erected quickly for hunting. They are extremely handy and durable. They are very effective at concealing boat, hunters, and gear from ducks' view. Their only drawbacks are price (several hundred dollars) and some complication in installation.

Duck Blinds

Many hunters build their own boat blinds, and designs and materials vary widely. Some collapse for running. Others are fixed upright. Some use only conduit framing, wire, and camou-

flage materials. Others have sides of plywood, fiberglass, aluminum, or cloth. Designs and materials are limited only by their creators' imaginations.

Some boat blind owners cover their blinds with natural vegetation. Others make use of such camo covers as net-ting, tarp, burlap, and grass mats. A combi-nation of camo mate-rials is desirable. An underlying tarp draped in camo net

Boat blind aesthetics: Camo netting conceals this boat blind (above), while another uses more natural materials.

and topped off with natural vegetation will totally cover a boat and its occupants, and it will do the best job at blending them into natural surroundings.

Weight is a major consideration when designing a boat blind. A boat blind should be as lightweight as possible both for safety and convenience.

A second consideration is the collapsible-fixed option. A collapsible blind is better for operating the boat—allowing easy entry, visibility while running, etc. Also, a collapsible blind is strongly recommended for hunting in flooded timber and brush, since it won't catch on low-hanging limbs.

On the other hand, a fixed-upright boat blind is fine for hunting big lakes and rivers, assuming the boat driver can see to steer. Just keep the center of gravity low so the boat won't be top-heavy.

A third category of boat blinds are factory-made boats designed and built specifically for waterfowl hunting. With these craft, boat and blind are one in the same. The sides of the boat angle up to screen hunters inside. An open shooting hole runs the length of the boat, from bow to stern. These boats typically have built-in storage for decoys, guns, and other gear. They are best on rivers and lakes where open water facilitates easy running. Because of their heavy weight, they are at a disadvantage in shallow backwaters and heavy cover.

Like a number of other boats built especially for waterfowling, the Duck Boat comes with built-in camouflage and a blind apparatus that pops up to conceal hunters

When possible, boat blind hunters should take advantage of natural cover for camouflage. After setting out the decoys, run the boat a few yards into reeds, brush, timber, etc., on the upwind or crosswind side of the hole, then set up the blind. This offers far better concealment than anchoring a boat blind in the open or at the edge of cover. (If possible, set up so the sun is behind you or off to the side, *not* directly in front of you.)

When I hunt from a boat blind, whenever it's possible I like to hide my boat beneath low overhanging branches of a tree. I position my boat next to the tree trunk and tie to it with stout rope to stabilize the shooting platform. Next I erect my portable blind, unrolling the cover to completely conceal the boat. Then I take limb pruners and trim away any limbs hanging toward the decoys that might impede shooting. However, I leave as much natural cover remaining as I can, especially overhead, to help blend the boat blind into the surroundings.

One highly desirable feature in a boat blind is a dry storage box to hold extra gear: life vests, spotlight, rope, portable heater, food, extra shells, pruners, a small ax, etc. Also, boat blind hunters should always carry a fire starting kit, signal devices, and other safety or survival gear in case an emergency arises. I also carry a complete set of clothing—from underwear to parka and cap—sealed in a plastic canoe bag and tucked in the storage box. This way, if a hunter takes an unexpected dunking he can change into warm, dry clothes before hypothermia sets in.

Other Portable Blinds

Other types of portable blinds are available to freelance hunters. Some are factory made, while others can be fashioned on site from simple materials that are readily available.

Hunter using Poke Boat in flooded rice field.

Sneak boats, layout boats, and kayaks are "movable pits" that allow hunters to disappear in broad open areas (flooded fields, mudflats, river sandbars, etc.). Such a boat can be towed or paddled to a desired hunting spot, then the hunter camouflages it (if necessary) and climbs inside to await the ducks' arrival.

Field layout blinds are highly effective for hunting both ducks and geese. These one-man ground blinds can be positioned exactly where birds have been feeding or resting, then camouflaged with straw, weeds, bean stubble, etc. Some models have spring-loaded panels that fold in to conceal the hunter's

This portable blind is designed to look like a natural tree stump.

body, but which spring open with the slightest nudge to allow for unencumbered shooting.

Various other portable commercial blinds are available: hay bale blinds, float tubes, pop-up blinds, etc., that can be adapted to a wide range of settings. Mail order catalogs that cater to waterfowl hunters will have several from which to choose. Most of these blinds have been developed by ardent hunters to meet personal needs, then taken to the market because of their effectiveness.

On-the-Spot Blinds

In some situations, a freelance duck hunter may wish to fashion a quick on-site blind where other types of portable blinds aren't available. This is possible using materials he can boat or tote in or collect in the field.

One example of such a blind is a camouflage net strung between poles cut on-site. When extreme cold temperatures freeze local marshes and flooded fields, I shift my hunting to large

On-site blinds can be fashioned in a variety of ways; all that's required is elbow work and ingenuity.

rivers where current keeps the water open. When I find an eddy pocket where ducks are resting, I sometimes set up on the bank nearby. I build a temporary blind by cutting saplings, pushing them in the mud in a half circle and spreading a camo net around them. Then I use brush, cane, or other natural vegetation to knit the blind into the surroundings. The steep riverbank shields me from behind. Also, if possible, I set up beneath overhanging trees or weeds to provide overhead cover. I've had some of the best hunts of my life huddled behind such makeshift blinds.

Other on-site blind options are to carry a roll of chicken wire and weave cane and weeds through the wire; to carry rolled burlap or grass mats and erect them with poles; to pile up driftwood or rocks; or simply to hide among trees, weeds, or whatever natural cover is available. In this regard, freelance hunters should carry a hand axe or pruners in their boat or backpack to cut such cover on-site.

With any portable blind, hunters must be aware of the necessity of having overhead cover as well as side cover. When ducks are sailing overhead, it's easy for them to spot hunters who are exposed from above. But if hunters are screened by overhead cover and resultant shadows, ducks flying over probably won't spot them. (Shadows are some of the best natural camouflage a duck hunter can use.)

Positioning a Duck Blind

Positioning a blind—permanent or temporary—in the right spot is crucial to its effectiveness. As I mentioned earlier,

Duck Blinds

Walter L. Williams III, Monroe, LA

"Camouflage Face and Hands to Hide from Ducks"

Hunters who hunt from pit blinds in open fields must take extra precautions to keep ducks from seeing their face and hands, says Walter L. Williams III. Williams has flown over his pit in north-central Louisiana while it was occupied by friends, and he was surprised at how uncovered faces and hands showed up in the pit opening. "Those big 'pie faces' stood out like you wouldn't believe, and so did the hands. This made me realize how easy it is for ducks to see hunters, and it convinced me of the necessity to put so much camouflage on the shooting hole flaps that you can't see through them.

The caller is the only person who should be exposed," Williams continues. "Everybody else should stay under cover and absolutely avoid looking up until it's time to shoot. Also, hunters who are wading outside blinds should use headnets and camo gloves to cover these exposed skin areas. I know that just taking these simple precautions will help a hunter bag more ducks."

hunters should consider such factors as sun direction, wind direction, terrain topography, and natural vegetation when deciding where to build or set up a blind.

If possible, never face a blind toward the rising sun. Looking into the sun restricts hunters' vision and makes it difficult to see colors on incoming ducks and thus distinguish between species and sexes. Also, hunters' faces reflecting sunlight are easy for ducks to see and avoid. Instead, set up with the rising sun to the back or side of the blind if wind direction and terrain features are favorable.

Blinds should be positioned to face downwind or crosswind. Ducks are like airplanes in that they land upwind. They will come head-on to a blind facing downwind or from the side of a blind facing crosswind. Ducks approaching from these directions will offer better shooting than those coming in from over the back of the blind.

Setting up a temporary blind for a particular wind is easy given the blind's portability. Take a wind reading, then position the blind upwind or crosswind of the decoys. However, since permanent blinds are harder or impossible to move, they should be positioned to take advantage of prevailing wind directions.

For instance, prevailing winds on a pothole where I frequently hunt in Kentucky are from the northwest and southwest. Thus my partners and I built our blind on the southwest edge of the pothole, facing northeast. With this position, ducks landing into a southwest wind will come straight into our faces. Ducks landing into a northwest wind will come from the right side of the blind, flying to our left. And the sun rises in the southeast and travels across the end and back of the blind through the course of the day. Its rays never fall directly into the front of the blind.

Final Word on Blinds

It's not a stretch to categorize duck blinds as a type of folk art. Blinds take many forms. They reflect the creativity, ingenuity, and energy of their builders. They are constructed from a broad range of materials. Collectively they are amazing in that so many different designs have been created to serve the same function.

Duck blinds are also reflections of their owner's personality. Every blind carries its builder's signature in some way, his special touch in layout or construction or camouflage. Part of the fun of duck hunting is dreaming up new ways to make blinds better, then transforming these ideas into reality.

And finally, each new duck blind is a monument to optimism. Each blind is built upon the hope that when fall arrives and the north wind blows, when frost starts wrapping the countryside under nightly blankets, and when new ducks begin arriving from up the flyway, its rewards will far outweigh the expense and effort it took to build it. With some luck, a new blind will become a center for exciting hunting action, for building memories with family and friends, and for playing out waterfowling's wonderful traditions for another season.

Chapter Six

Scouting, Intelligence Gathering

from the distance, the cloud of mallards resembled a dust storm blowing over the South Dakota landscape. It stretched across much of the horizon, partially screening out the thin light of the setting sun. This great flight had risen from a marsh somewhere to the north, and it had set its sights on one of the many freshly-harvested cornfields that lay scattered across the countryside.

My two partners and I stood on the road by our Suburban and watched with binoculars. We were spellbound by this spectacle. Who could guess how many ducks there were? Ten thousand? Maybe 20,000, or more?

But instead of speculating on numbers, we wondered where these birds had come from, and we devised a plan to find out. We'd be back the next morning before dawn, towing a boat with decoys. These ducks would fly out to the fields again at first light, and hopefully we'd be able to backtrack them to their roost. Then, while the ducks were feeding, we'd launch the boat, find a hunting spot, and toss out our spread to await their return. If our game plan worked, we could be in for one of the best shoots of our lives.

It did, and we were! When the sun started rising, the ducks came again, one group after another in almost continual succession. We raced along backroads beneath them, going the opposite way. After a half hour of driving, we watched the last remnants of the great feeding flight lift off from a marsh that spanned a hundred acres or more. To our glee, a sign by the roadway read Public Hunting Area.

Sometimes there's no substitute for firsthand knowledge of the ducks' movements.

In another hour, we had our boat blind hidden in cattails and our decoys scattered across an open hole that was ringed by matted duck feathers. We'd loaded our shotguns and were piddling with other gear when we heard a rushing noise like a jet at low level. Before we could react, 25 mallards plopped down in our spread. They flushed when we stood up to shoot. Four greenheads splashed while the remainder made good their escape.

Soon another flight arrived, and another, and another. We finished our limits in a matter of minutes, then we huddled in the blind and enjoyed the spectacle. For the next two hours ducks were constantly overhead, sailing and calling and picking landing spots in the reedy marsh below. It was more than ample reward for the long drive and great effort we'd made to get here. All these ducks, and no other hunters.

Actually, this payoff came as a result of months of research before our trip ever started. Rule No. 1 in waterfowl hunting is to go where the birds are. The best blind, decoys, calling, shooting skills, retriever, and other trappings of this sport won't add up to success if there are no ducks to be had. All hunting gear and strategies are predicated on the assumption that ducks are present. If they're not, you're doomed to failure. Period.

Thus, scouting and collecting information about where ducks are is a critical step to success. Hunters should resolve to do the best scouting job they can, then follow through by tracking leads like detectives trying to break a difficult case.

This is true both for traveling hunters, as we were in South Dakota, and for those sticking close to home. Travelers must do everything they can to ensure that ducks will be where they're going when they're going there. In other words, they should plan so their travel coincides with the migration. Nothing is more disheartening than committing great time, expense, and energy to get to a distant hunting spot, then learning that the ducks have already passed through, or that they haven't arrived yet from up north. Sure, weather can't be controlled, and timing of peak migration varies from year to year. But good investigators can determine the average time of peak migration, then hope for the best.

Chapter Six

In the same vein, stay-at-home hunters should scout continually to keep up with duck concentrations in their home area. Birds will move overnight when food or water conditions change. They can literally be here today in big numbers, then gone somewhere else tomorrow. Hunters who keep up with the birds' movements can stay in the action.

Two Tiers of Scouting

Scouting can be "primary" and "secondary." Primary scouting involves actually going afield to track ducks' movements within a given area. This obviously takes sizeable investments in time and personal effort.

Secondary scouting can be done from home, specifically by telephone and computer. This includes keeping in touch with a network of other hunters to share information. It also includes collecting such details as river or lake levels, duck counts on refuges, harvest figures on controlled hunting areas, and any other clues as to where ducks are working and where hunting might be best.

Here is an example of how primary and secondary scouting can combine to yield a good hunt. A few years back a friend and I were hunting in a swamp in west Kentucky, and action was slow. We'd seen several hundred ducks, but they were high and all flying northeast. "Something's going on we don't know about," I commented. We left our spot at noon, and I returned home determined to unravel the mystery of where the ducks were headed.

I phoned a couple of hunting acquaintances, but with no luck. Then I logged onto the Army Corps of Engineers Web site on the Internet, checked area river levels, and discovered that the lower Ohio River was at flood stage and still rising. That was the answer! The ducks we had seen were heading to the river to feed on freshly flooded corn and soybean fields. A quick call to another hunter who lived in this area confirmed this. The next morning my partner and I launched my portable boat blind on the river, and we had a limit of ducks before noon.

Binoculars are an important tool for locating and identifying ducks at a distance.

Just like in the military, good intelligence is essential to success in duck hunting. Without good intelligence you're left to the whims of chance. But through scouting, if you've ascertained that ducks are where you'll be hunting, you're at least assured of having a chance. The odds are lined up in your favor. Then your success depends on your other skills of picking a good hunting spot, setting decoys, hiding, calling, and shooting.

Timing the Migration

Like all wildlife, dabbling ducks' locations and daily movements are governed by natural conditions in their habitat. More specifically, where ducks can be found is determined by time of year and a combination of weather, food, cover, and disturbance conditions (primarily, hunting pressure). These birds are highly mobile, and they will move many miles overnight when conditions change.

Time of year is the first consideration. Most dabbling ducks will linger on northern nesting and staging grounds until early fall. Then they will begin migrating toward southern wintering grounds in all four major flyways. Timing of this migration depends on species of ducks and weather conditions. Some species (blue-winged teal, gadwall, pintails, etc.) migrate earlier than others (mallards, black ducks, green-winged teal). Early migrators may leave northern prairies at the first hint of seasonal change. Late migrators may linger until deep snow blankets grainfields and ice locks up potholes and open water.

When the migration is on, the day following a cold front can bring spectacular hunting.

Research shows that most dabbling ducks migrate as cold fronts stir strong northerly winds, which boost the birds' true airspeed. In calm air, mallards will fly 45 to 50 mph. Add a 20 to 40 mph tailwind, and they can cover greater southbound distances in much shorter time spans.

Urgency of the migration depends on the severity of winter's onset. A warm, gentle fall will lead to a trickle-down

migration, wherein ducks will linger up north longer and work
their way south in short stages. In contrast, an arctic blast with
strong, cold winds and heavy snow can trigger a "grand passage," with spectacular numbers of waterfowl migrating long
distances in one big push. Southern wintering grounds can be
barren one day and covered up with ducks the next day.

It's little wonder, then, that seasoned waterfowlers keep a
close check on weather patterns as fall progresses. Thanks to
emerging weather technologies, forecasts are more accurate
than ever, even a week or longer in advance. Monitoring weather patterns up the flyway is crucial in anticipating how the
migration is unfolding and when new ducks will arrive. When
the migration is on, the day following a cold frontal passage is
typically when new ducks will show up.

How Changing Conditions Affect
Daily Movements of Ducks in a Local Area
Daily movements of dabbling ducks within a given area are
influenced by weather, food and water conditions, and hunting pressure. When these conditions change, ducks may shift quickly to a
new area where feeding and resting conditions are more amenable.

For instance, dabbling ducks like to move to fresh, rising
water. During periods of stable weather, ducks may hold on a
refuge or some undisturbed resting area, and they might range
out several miles to feed. However, following a heavy rain,
these birds will typically vacate established feeding and resting
areas and fly to newly flooded areas where fresh food is available. Such a movement can occur in a matter of hours.

Chapter Six

Brent Carper, Jacksonville, AR

"Scouting by Airplane to Locate Ducks"

Duck hunting guide Brent Carper has a unique way of scouting and keeping up with duck movements. "A partner and I scout from the ducks' perspective," he explains. "We scout by air. We rent a small airplane and go up to look for concentrations of birds. It's amazing how much territory you can cover in a short period of time. Ducks move around a lot, but by scouting from the air we can usually relocate birds quickly. We scout in the late afternoon for hunting the following morning."

Carper says the trick is learning what to look for. "You won't usually see ducks on the water. Instead, you'll see them flying over treetops, or you'll see their wings flapping as they descend into timber—like a Wonder Duck. Another thing to look for is agitated water in both timber and fields. The more you do this, the better you'll become at spotting birds."

Carper scouts by air only as necessary to stay in birds. "When we find a concentration of ducks, we'll hunt them until they change locations, then we'll go find them again. We probably average flying twice a week, and we stay up about an hour per flight. My buddy and I split the cost, so the expense isn't too bad. Really, this is some of the best money I spend in duck hunting. Scouting from the air and being mobile allows us to stay in birds when other hunters are floundering."

(Biologists don't know how ducks communicate the discovery of new food sources, but "word" indisputably spreads quickly. A radio tracking study in Louisiana documented mass movements of ducks up to 300 miles overnight to reach freshly flooded rice and soybean fields.)

This is why hunters should keep daily tabs on water and food conditions in their hunting area and be ready to take advantage of new opportunities that arise. Hunting is usually best the first day or two that new feeding areas are flooded. Ducks will head upstream when floodwaters are breaking out, then will follow the flood crest back downstream when water begins falling.

Conversely, in a prolonged drought or freeze, dabbling ducks will raft up on big lakes or free-flowing rivers—wherever they can find open water. They will feed early and late in dry fields, then return to the water to loaf during midday.

Hunting pressure is unlikely to cause ducks to change locations if other conditions are static, but it can certainly have a detrimental effect on hunter success. Heavily pressured birds are more cautious. They become call- and blind-shy. Heavy hunting pressure causes them to feed more at night and less during the day.

Hunters hunting in areas where pressure is heavy and new ducks are scarce might be better off trying somewhere else where ducks might not be as plentiful (get away from the refuge) but where the birds that are there aren't as educated as to the purposes of decoy spreads and sweet-sounding calls.

Networking with Other Hunters

To repeat, a hunter's challenge is to keep up with duck movements and be in the right hunting spot at the right time.

In this regard, collecting and maintaining information sources is crucial. Businessmen call it "networking." Hunters should network with other hunters to keep up with changing conditions and duck movements. By maintaining contact with hunters in different areas, you can collect reliable reports by placing a few quick phone calls.

Chapter Six

"Hunt the Middle of the Lake for New Ducks"

66When new ducks are coming into a lake, they will usually hit the center of the lake since they're unfamiliar with the refuges or little out-of-the-way places where local ducks sit," says guide and outfitter Mike McClelland. "When I know there's a migration in progress, I scout late in the afternoon, and I'll go where I can watch the center of the lake or marsh. Then if I see ducks working, I'll return before dawn the next morning to hunt. If it's a pothole lake, I'll set up in the opening closest to the center. If it's a reservoir, I'll look for a long point or an island in the middle of the open water. I'll guarantee, these are the places where shooting will be best until those new ducks learn their way around."

During hunting season, I spend a considerable amount of time on the phone. I maintain some two dozen trustworthy contacts, and I stay in constant touch with them. If birds get scarce in one area, I call around to get reports from other areas to determine where to go.

Cell phones have raised this capability even higher. I now take a cell phone on each hunt, and my buddies do likewise. If ducks aren't flying, I'll check with other hunters to see if I should move. And if ducks *are* flying, I'll call my partners to alert them.

The Internet is another valuable source of information about duck concentrations and movements. Some waterfowl refuges post weekly census counts. Some state wildlife agencies do likewise. Private Web sites offer daily hunter reports and opportunities to contact and chat with other hunters. Again, Army Corps of Engineers Web sites provide river stage information.

Here's the bottom line on collecting information through telephone contacts and the Internet. The hunter who is both persistent and imaginative in developing and maintaining good contacts will bag more ducks. (This assumes he has the capability to hunt different areas when he determines that ducks are using them.) Few places are good day after day. As duck concentrations shift around, hunters should shift with them. Those who do, based on reliable scouting and information, will be rewarded by consistent shooting and the satisfaction of a job well done.

Building a Map Library

Maps are extremely useful in following leads, planning hunts, finding access, checking terrain features, etc. Road maps, topographic maps, aerial maps, and others can help a hunter get into an area and determine where ducks should be. This is why waterfowl hunters should build and maintain a map library of their favorite spots, or potential favorites.

The Internet can be a major aide in doing this. Information is available on-line to obtain virtually any maps offered to the public. Map acquisition via the Internet is both easy and fast.

For instance, the U.S. Geological Survey is the official mapper for the federal government. Through this agency, duck hunters can obtain topographic maps, photo image maps, and other types of maps. All these maps can be purchased on-line through the Survey's official Web site: www.usgs.gov. Topo maps cost $4 each. A $5 service charge is added for each order.

Chapter Six

Several private map companies offer topographic maps on-line, and they also sell such maps as state atlases, GPS coordinate topographic maps, and 3-D topographic map programs. Two examples are the DeLorme company (www.delorme.com) and Maptech, Inc. (www.maptech.com). Maptech also offers free on-line topographic maps via its MapServer feature. Map resolution of downloaded-printed maps isn't as good as that of original maps.

Brad Harris, Neosho, MO

"Finding Holes Can Lead to Quality Shooting"

Pro hunter Brad Harris specializes on scouting up little potholes and strip mine pits where ducks are thick and which other hunters have overlooked. "These little honey holes are scattered all over the country," Harris says. "You really have to look to find them. I scout by car, boat, and on foot. I religiously use binoculars and a spotting scope to watch where ducks are going in. Then I'll mark the spot and go to it to see exactly where the ducks are and how to hunt it."

Harris says the wetter the weather, the more of these potholes he finds. "And when I find a good one, I'll remember the conditions, and if they come up again in a future season, that spot will be good again. So over the years I've built up an inventory of these places," he explains.

Harris says a good example are the strip mine pits near his home on the Kansas-Missouri border. "We've got a lot of old stripper pits that are surrounded by thick, grown-up woods. When the hunting season is in, I'll watch from a high vantage where I can observe ducks moving about. When I see a flight lock up and drop into a pit, I'll mark it and then hike in for a close-up look. I've found some great spots and had some super shooting over the years by doing this."

Aerial photo maps are available free of charge via the Web site www.TerraServer.com, part of the Microsoft Network. On this site, browsers can call up and print enlarged aerial photo maps of virtually any location in the U.S. Again, resolution isn't as good as on original maps.

Maps showing public land holdings are available through all land management agency Web sites. Some state wildlife agencies offer sportsman's atlases, which show management areas, boat ramps, and other useful information. River charts and reservoir maps can be purchased through the Army Corps of Engineers, U.S. Bureau of Reclamation, and TVA.

County highway maps show most secondary roads and are a help to hunters in navigating through backcountry. Many state highway/transportation departments sell these. Contact information is available through state government Web sites.

Chapter Seven

Shotguns and Loads

I'd been loaned the shotgun by a company representative who wanted me to give it a try. It was a new-model autoloader with an alluring look, several fancy features, and a lot of hype. It also had an atmospheric price tag, but that didn't affect me since I'd be field-testing the shotgun, then shipping it back to the factory when the season was over.

I was heading to prairie Canada for a combination duck-goose hunt, and when I packed my gun case, discretion reigned. The new shotgun went in first, but I added my old regular pumpgun as a backup. I've learned from experience that shooting shotguns can be like making conversation at a dinner party. Talking to strangers may be uneasy, but my old companion and I are comfortable with each other. We share several inside jokes.

The first morning the new shotgun performed well. It felt unfamiliar against my shoulder, which was to be expected, as new guns take some getting used to. But it shot and ejected empties and dropped birds as I'd also expected. Back in camp, I gave it a perfunctory wipe-down, put it in the gun rack, and forgot it.

The next morning the weather was colder, and a stiff wind was blowing fine grit across the barley field. After a couple of salvos, the new shotgun got balky. The bolt wouldn't close after ejecting the first hull. I manually cycled shells through the gun. I blew into the receiver. I wiped it with my shirttail and looked for impediments that would keep the action from working. Still, despite my best in-the-field gunsmithing, I was a one-shot Charlie.

Later that morning, back in camp, the conversation with my old scarred-up shotgun was a little hat-in-hand. It went something like this. "Hello, old friend. I missed you this morning. No, she didn't work out. She wore a lot of makeup, but it rubbed off fast. Yes, I know we've been down this road before. Yes, I know I should have learned this lesson already. No, you've never let me down—always true-blue. Yes, I promise, tomorrow you'll go to the dance, and she'll stay home. You're not real pretty, but you sure can boogie."

OK, so this conversation is hokey, but the relationship between hunters and their duck guns can get personal. Shotguns are more than inert tools of metal and wood (or plastic). They're partners with personality and even sensitivity. A hunter and his shotgun share a history. They've been places together, worked together, endured hardships, and shared achievements. A veteran hunter knows his shotgun's touch. The two are comfortable with each other. The hunter leads, and his "dance partner" follows fluidly from seasons of practice.

Shooting is an integral part of duck hunting. Each hunter must select a suitable gun and load, then learn to use them efficiently. A hunter must also know how to take care of his shotgun so it will provide reliable service. Following are guidelines for choosing a gun, customizing it, cleaning it, choosing loads, and learning to be a capable shot in the broad spectrum of duck hunting situations.

Shotgun Actions

Autoloader, pump, hinge action, bolt—which shotgun action is best for hunting dabbling ducks? Redheads, blonds, or brunettes—which are prettier? Both questions have the same answer: It depends on personal preference. Beauty lies in the eye of the beholder. Choice of shotgun actions is strictly a matter of individual inclination. There is no such thing as "best," but rather "best for me."

However, there are several factors to consider when choosing a shotgun action for duck hunting. A hunter should determine whether two shots are enough, or whether he'd prefer to have three. How reliable will the gun be in tough hunting conditions? Is recoil a factor? What about price? Following are guidelines to help hunters make the choice that best suits their personal needs and desires.

Autoloaders (semi-automatics). The name describes the action of this highly popular style of shotgun. The gun is loaded manually, then when the first shell is fired, subsequent shells are fed, fired, and ejected by simply pulling the trigger. Everything is done automatically by harnessing energy from recoil and/or expansion of gases resulting from powder ignition. Quick second and third shots are readily available. Shooters can stay on target and continue shooting. Also, the working of the action absorbs some of the recoil of autoloaders, especially in gas-operated models. The downside of autoloaders is the complexity of their actions and the greater likelihood that they will jam if not cleaned properly or if exposed to ice, snow, dust, cold, etc.

Browning's semi-automatic Gold Hunter is one of many popular autoloaders.

Many veteran duck hunters wouldn't dream of going afield without their trusty pumpgun. This hunter's Winchester Model 12 is among the best ever made.

Autoloaders, especially gas-operated models, must be cleaned religiously to be kept in reliable working order.

Pumps (slide actions). Again, the name describes the action of these 3-shot shotguns. A pump is operated by pumping a sliding forearm back and forth to eject spent shells and load fresh ones. When the forearm returns to the forward position, the bolt locks in place until the trigger is pulled or the action is released by pushing a depressible button. Pump shotguns are highly revered among duck hunters for their reliability. This action is very simple; there are few moving parts to malfunction. Pumpguns are also very easy to break down for cleaning or repair. Another positive factor is their price. Pumps are significantly less expensive than autoloaders. They are an excellent choice for practical, budget-minded duck hunters. The only negative is the chance for some interruption in swing when working the pump action between shots. However, with minimal practice, hunters can learn to work pumps without thinking or pulling off target. In the hands of a veteran, a pump is as fast and effective as an autoloader. Another negative is that pumps have slightly more felt recoil than autoloaders.

Hinge action. Hinge action shotguns include three styles: over-under, side-by-side, and single barrel. These shotguns "break down" by working a lever on the back of the receiver. The barrels open downward on a hinged mechanism, exposing the chambers for manual loading. Then, when shells are inserted, the barrels

Some hunters choose over-unders for the feel and traditions associated with these sleek double guns.

rels are snapped back into place for shooting. In over-under models, one barrel is aligned directly beneath another. In side-by-sides, two barrels are joined in the same plane with a sighting rib between them. And a single barrel is just that—one barrel, one shot. The main advantage of hinge action shotguns is their reliability. There are very few mechanical parts that can break. Another advantage of two-barrel models is the option to use two different chokes and select which choke to use first. For instance, for shooting over decoys, a hunter might choose a more open choke (improved-cylinder or modified) for the first shot and a more constricted choke (modified or full) for the second shot. One disadvantage is these guns' inability to deliver a second (with single barrel) or third (with over-under, side-by-side) follow-up shot. Another disadvantage is sharper recoil with heavy loads. And a third disadvantage in over-unders and side-by-sides is high price because of the extensive custom work required in their manufacture. Hinge action shotguns aren't nearly as popular among duck hunters as autoloaders and pumps, but many over-unders and side-by-sides are used by shooters who prefer their "feel" and who enjoy the tradition associated with these shotguns. Very few single barrels are used in duck hunting because of their obvious limitation to one shot.

Bolt action. Bolt action shotguns are similar to bolt action rifles: spent loads are ejected and new loads inserted into the chamber by manually working a bolt. This action is slow and cumbersome, requiring a shooter to take his hand off the trigger between shots to work the action. For this reason, bolt action shotguns are rarely used by duck hunters. This shotgun is better suited to types of hunting where quick follow-up shots aren't needed.

Best Gauges/Loads for Dabbling Ducks

For all practical purposes, duck hunters are limited to 10-, 12-, and 20-gauge shotguns by the availability of non-toxic loads. (A very minimal selection of .410, 28-, and 16-gauge non-toxic loads is available, but the .410 and 28-gauge are too small and light to bag ducks efficiently except at the closest ranges, and the 16-gauge has all but disappeared from the American duck hunting scene.)

Far and away, the 12-gauge is the most popular gauge among dabbler hunters. The 10-gauge is used by a few duck hunters who desire maximum firepower or who pass-shoot at long ranges. And the 20-gauge is used by many younger hunters or expert shooters who are shooting at close-to-medium ranges and who prefer the lighter recoil and challenge of this lighter gauge.

In 12-gauge, non-toxic loads are available in 2¾-, 3-, and 3½-inch lengths. In 10-gauge, non-toxic loads are available only in 3½-inch length. In 20-gauge, non-toxic loads are available in 2¾- and 3-inch lengths.

In general, the bigger the gauge and the longer the casing, the more powder and shot a load holds. In other words, a 10-gauge 3½-inch magnum

Modern shotshells are virtually leak-proof, and perform well in the extreme conditions encountered by duck hunters.

shotshell holds a much heavier (i.e., stronger) load than a 20-gauge 3-inch—1¼ ounces of shot versus 1 ounce of shot.

A universal rule for selecting loads for dabbling ducks is to go with heavier loads of bigger pellets for longer average shots, and lighter loads of smaller pellets for closer shots. For instance, pass-shooters may opt for a 3½-inch 10- or 12-gauge load with steel BBs or BBBs. A better choice for shooting over decoys would be a 12-gauge 3- or 2¾-inch load with No.3 steel shot. By far the most popular shotshell used by duck hunters today is the 12-gauge 3-inch magnum loaded with 1⅛ ounces of steel shot.

All major shotshell manufacturers now also offer non-toxic loads that are alternatives to steel-shot loads. These loads contain pellets made from bismuth, tungsten, nickel, iron, and various alloys of these metals. These pellets are heavier than steel pellets, and they carry more retained energy. They perform similar to lead shot in terms of knockdown power and pattern density. Also, they retain their energy better at longer ranges than equivalent-sized steel pellets.

The problem with these new non-toxic loads is their cost—close to $2 per round. They are sold in boxes of 10 instead of 25 to avoid sticker shock. In coming seasons, competition among manufacturers may lower the price of these exotics slightly, but not much. The high expense in purchasing these raw metals and transforming them into pellets won't go away, so the cost

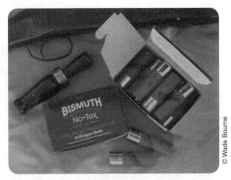

Some hunters are willing to pay more for the added performance of non-toxic loads.

of a box of 10 of these alternative non-toxic loads will likely remain in the $17 to $20 range.

So are these new non-toxics worth their lofty price? No question, they have more knockdown power than steel loads. However, premium steel loads are entirely sufficient for consistent clean kills on ducks to 50 yards. My recommendation is this: If cost is a consideration, use premium steel loads in No.3 or No.2 shot for hunting over decoys. For longer ranges (pass-shooting, jump-shooting, open-water hunting, etc.), go with steel BBs, or if you can afford it, switch to one of the new non-toxics in No.4 shot. And if cost is no object and you want absolute top performance, use the new non-toxics in all situations (No.5s over decoys, No.4s or No.2s for pass-shooting).

Commonsense Advice on Shotgun Chokes

Shotgun chokes are the subject of much confusion among duck hunters, especially since steel-shot loads came on the scene.

A choke is a constriction in the end of the shotgun muzzle that is intended to "squeeze" a shot charge so that it will provide a denser pattern at longer range. Supposedly, the tighter the choke, the better the downrange performance.

However, steel loads came out with warnings from manufacturers to shoot them through more open chokes (improved-cylinder or modified instead of full). The idea was that since steel pellets were harder than lead pellets, they wouldn't compress as they flowed through the choke. Thus larger steel pellets, especially, might cause ring bulging in the barrel at the entry of the choke. Also, prevailing thought was that poor patterns could result from steel pellets jamming through the muzzle and jostling each other upon exit.

The truth of these theories is...maybe, and maybe not. Performance differs with each individual shotgun, choke, and load. Also, most modern shotguns come with hardened choke tubes that eliminate the possibility of ring bulging. Some hardened full-choked shotguns will deliver tight, uniform patterns of steel shot at extended ranges.

The only way a shooter can know how his gun-choke-load will perform is to test them. Spend an afternoon at a local gun club, and test-fire several patterns at standard distances (40 and 50 yards). Try your favorite duck load with improved-cylinder, modified, and full chokes (or with the built-in choke if you don't have screw-in tubes), and see which one delivers the densest, most uniform pattern. When the afternoon is over, all confusion will be gone, and you will know for certain which choke gives the best performance with your chosen load.

Since alternative non-toxic loads perform similar to lead loads, old rules about shotgun chokes apply. For closer shooting, use more open chokes. An improved-cylinder choke is better for close-in shots over decoys. For longer shooting, use tighter chokes. A full choke is preferred by many pass-shooters, float-hunters, open-water hunters, etc. A modified choke is a good middle-of-the-road tube for all-around duck shooting. Still, patterning preferred loads through various chokes is a good idea to build knowledge and confidence in how they are performing.

One tip for using screw-in chokes: Always apply a small amount of choke tube lubricant on a tube's threads before screwing it into a shotgun barrel. This will prevent locked threads and the difficulty of removing a tube that is left installed for an extended time period.

Other Shotgun Features

Many new shotguns are available in a camouflage finish.

Duck hunters may wish to customize their shotguns by adding any of the following features to make them more efficient and convenient.

Camouflage finish. A camo finish will help a shotgun blend in. Shotguns may be purchased with a "dipped" camo job from the factory, or hunters may cover their guns with camouflage tape. However, leaving tape on a gun through a hunting season can lead to rust where moisture invades between the seams. A factory camouflage job is far superior to taping.

Matte finish. A matte finish is an alternative to the standard bluing on a shotgun's barrel and receiver. While bluing is shiny, a matte finish is non-glare. Also, a matte finish is more resistant to rubbing off in tough hunting conditions. The only downside to a matte finish is an aesthetic one: the gun won't have the glossy sheen that some shooters desire in a new shotgun. A matte finish may come on a new shotgun, or it can be applied by your local gunsmith.

Teflon finish. This is a third alternative in shotgun finishes that is available through some manufacturers' custom gun shops. A Teflon coating is similar to a matte finish in appearance (black, no-shine). Its purpose is to repel water. A Teflon-coated shotgun won't rust. Therefore, it takes less in-the-field maintenance. Having a shotgun Teflon-coated is expensive, but it is a very nice convenience.

Synthetic stock, forearm. A synthetic (plastic) stock and forearm are options to standard wood parts. A synthetic stock and forearm won't dent, scratch, crack, or swell. They are extremely practical options for a waterfowl shotgun. Again, the

Don Wright, Hopkinsville, KY

"Don't Shoot the Most Obvious Duck in Flight"

Longtime waterfowler Don Wright says that when a flight of ducks sails into shotgun range, many hunters have the tendency to focus on the closest, lowest, easiest shot, and this invariably causes two or three shooters in the blind to shoot at the same bird. Instead, Wright intentionally takes a trailer on his first shot. "I'll pick out a duck back in the flight, maybe one that's higher than the birds landing in the decoys," he explains. "This way, I'm rarely competing with other hunters, and also my gun is in the right plane to take flaring birds on the second and third shot. If other hunters will do this, they'll be more efficient with their shooting, and they'll have the satisfaction of knowing they downed ducks that nobody else was shooting at."

only drawback is the loss of aesthetics in terms of the beauty and feel of natural wood. Synthetic stocks and forearms are available in either camouflage or muted black.

Sling. Adding a sling to a shotgun is a practical convenience to duck hunters who will be wading through flooded timber, swamps, or sloughs. Being able to sling a shotgun over a shoulder makes carrying easier and frees up hands to tote decoys and other gear. Adjustable padded slings of waterproof fabric are recommended. Slings are available in a variety of modern camouflage patterns.

Recoil pad. A recoil pad is helpful in cutting down on felt recoil from heavy duck loads. Some shotguns come from the factory with a recoil pad installed. Or a hunter can have a recoil pad installed by his gunsmith. This is a good option, since the gunsmith can cut and fit the stock and recoil pad to the shooter's exact measurements. (These measurements should be taken while a hunter is wearing his standard duck hunting clothing. It's better to have a stock that is too short in light clothing than too long in heavy clothing.)

Ventilated rib. A ventilated rib is a raised sighting plane that extends down the length of the barrel from the receiver to the muzzle. A ventilated rib's purpose is to make sighting easier and more natural for the shooter. It provides a better visual reference for tracking moving targets. Ventilated ribs are available on factory shotguns or from your local gunsmith.

Barrel length. "Thirty-inch full" used to be the standard shotgun barrel for many waterfowl hunters, but no longer. Interchangeable choke tubes now allow hunters to use the choke of their choice in a shorter, more "user-friendly" barrel length. In my opinion, the best overall choice is a 28-inch barrel with screw-in chokes. The 28-inch barrel has plenty length and weight for smooth tracking of targets, but it's not cumbersome. Some hunters who hunt in up-close settings (flooded timber, marshes) might prefer a 26-inch barrel for its faster pointing and swinging.

Cleaning Your Shotgun

Keeping a shotgun clean is imperative in maintaining its good working order and preserving its appearance and value. Many duck hunts are conducted in tough conditions. Shotguns get wet, muddy, and gritty. Especially with automatics, not cleaning them properly can lead to malfunctions (which always seem to occur when ducks are flying best). Also, neglecting to clean a wet shotgun can result in rust and metal pitting, which makes a tramp out of a beauty queen.

So make a habit of cleaning your shotgun after each hunting trip. This might just be a "wipe down" after a day in a permanent blind where conditions were easy, or it might be a total "break-down cleaning" after a hard freelance hunt where a shotgun was "drug through the mud." Whichever, take good care of your shotgun, and it'll take care of you.

When doing a wipe down, the first step is thoroughly rubbing all exposed metal parts with a clean, dry rag to remove moisture, perspiration salts, etc. Next apply a thin coating of WD-40 or similar cleaner. Understand that WD-40 is *not* a lubricant. It is a *penetrant* that removes water, oil, etc. ("WD" stands for "water displacement.") After spraying, wipe the WD-40 off, then rub the gun down one more time with an oily rag for lubrication. Three-In-One oil or a synthetic gun oil (*not* silicon or Teflon-based) is the best choice in gun lubricants.

All hunters should know how to break their shotguns down, removing the barrel, forearm, bolt, and trigger assembly from the receiver. This exposes internal parts for a more thorough cleaning. Don't wait for hunting season to learn how to do this; practice in the preseason. New shotguns come with manuals that instruct in proper break-down procedure. Owners of older guns can get instruction from friends who own the same make shotgun or from their local gunsmith.

Once the bolt is out, spray it with carburetor cleaner or soak it in mineral spirits to wash grime away. Clean the trigger assembly with an artist's brush dipped in mineral spirits, brushing through the trigger group. Then clean and dry the bolt and trigger assembly with a can of compressed air (available at auto parts stores).

While the bolt and trigger assembly are removed, clean the inside of the receiver with a spray solvent, then dry thoroughly. Add a drop of oil to the groove where the bolt slides out. Again, do not use silicon or Teflon-based oil, since this oil will congeal in cold weather and make the action sluggish.

Duck hunters who use gas-operated automatic shotguns must be especially faithful about regular and proper cleaning. With these guns, gases from fired shells are vented into the gas cylinder to work the action. Carbon buildup is a byproduct of this sequence. If carbon clogs the gas entry ports, or if the gas piston housing gets coated with carbon, the piston will bind, and the action will be hindered and eventually fail.

When cleaning a gas-operated shotgun, do not use oil on the gas cylinder, as oil will combine with the carbon to become gummy. Instead, remove the gas piston assembly, and clean thoroughly with a good solvent. Mineral spirits is best, but gasoline or other carbon-eating solvent will work in an emergency. If carbon buildup is especially heavy, use an old butter knife or a similar tool to scrape it off.

Most wood stocks come with a plastic coating. If this plastic cracks, water can seep in and cause swelling, discoloration, and more cracking. This is why, if a stock gets wet, it must be dried thoroughly. If water invades a crack, blow-dry it with a hair dryer. Then after the stock is thoroughly dry, seal the crack with clear fingernail polish or with a polyurethane wipe-on sealant.

Another way to prevent water invasion in the stock is to remove the butt plate or recoil pad and apply a polyurethane spray liberally to the butt of the stock. This area is frequently left uncoated on shotguns shipped from the factory.

One good idea related to cleaning is to check the bore before each hunt to make sure it's not plugged. Sometimes a barrel will become unintentionally plugged with mud or some other foreign object. A shotgun that is fired in this condition will result in a fractured barrel. I was in a blind once with a hunter who shot at the first duck of the morning and blew six inches off the end of his barrel. Subsequent investigation revealed that he had uncased his shotgun before putting it in the boat. Then the gun had slid forward, and the barrel plugged with snow. A quick check of the bore before loading the shotgun would have prevented this accident.

Cases for Duck Guns

All duck guns should be cased when transporting, both for protection of the gun and for safety purposes. (My aforementioned friend wouldn't have blown his barrel off if he'd kept his shotgun encased until he arrived at the blind.) Many types and styles of cases are available. I prefer those made from camouflaged Cordura and that feature flota-

A proper gun case is essential for keeping your shotgun clean, dry, and functional.

tion padding. In such a case, a gun dropped over the side of a boat will stay on the surface.

An alternative to a gun case is a "gun sock" that is impregnated with silicone. These socks are soft and supple. They don't offer the protection of padded cases described above, but they do provide a measure of defense against rough handling. Their main benefit is the silicone that keeps a light coating on the shotgun to prevent rust. Silicon on the *outside* of the gun is OK. (For maximum protection, keep a shotgun inside a gun sock inside a padded gun case.)

One note about gun cases: Never leave your shotgun inside a case for long periods after a hunt. An encased shotgun can't dry out, and will therefore rust. This is especially true when a cold shotgun is brought inside. As it warms, condensation will occur. If this condensation is retained inside a case, a fine shotgun can turn into a rust bucket in short order. (It's a good idea to keep a couple of bags of desiccant [moisture remover] in a gun case when traveling or if shotguns must be encased for extended periods.)

Tips for Being a Good Duck Shot

Telling someone how to be a good duck shot is like telling a golfer how to improve his swing or a tennis player his stroke. It takes more than words. Becoming a good shot starts with having a shotgun that fits. Then it requires qualified shooting instruction and lots of practice. Also, a measure of God-given athletic skill—hand-eye coordination—is a blessing in dropping birds consistently.

A qualified shooting instructor can get you started on the right track.

Start by purchasing a shotgun that feels comfortable, that mounts easily to your shoulder and points like an extension of your arm. As in the story at the beginning of this chapter, a shotgun should be like a good dance partner that flows smoothly with your lead. Most factory shotguns are built for the average-size shooter and may or may not feel right "off the rack." A qualified gunsmith can custom-fit a new shotgun to your exact measurements at minimal expense. (Again, make sure to check a new shotgun's fit when wearing hunting clothes, including parka.)

Mike Jordan, Moro IL

"Use Pre-Season Practice to Sharpen Shooting Eye"

Too many duck hunters make the mistake of leaving their shotguns in their gun closet until opening day, and not practicing with it is reflected in their shooting prowess, or lack of it. Mike Jordan, longtime employee of Winchester ammo and a 40-plus year duck hunter, advises getting a "shooting tune-up" on a sporting clays range before hunting season begins.

"Take the shotgun you hunt with, and ask the range operator if you can practice only on the stations applicable to duck hunting. You mostly need to shoot at incoming, descending targets and at high passing targets. Also, if the operator says it's OK, you might back up 10 to 15 yards from the shooting station to try some harder shots."

Jordan continues, "Just keep shooting these targets until you get the right sight picture and you're swinging through the targets when you shoot. It's amazing how just a little preseason practice will improve your shooting percentage when opening day rolls around."

Next I recommend taking a shooting course from a certified instructor. Sure, many fine duck shots never had a moment of instruction. They learned to hit birds on their own. However, I'd bet they would have become better shots *sooner* if they'd started out taking lessons. Learning how to mount, point, and swing a shotgun comes more easily through instruction from a qualified coach. Check at your local gun club to find such a person.

Then shoot, shoot, shoot! Good shots are made, not born. Any type of shooting will improve familiarity with your shotgun and increase hand-eye coordination. Skeet, trap, and hand-thrown targets offer good practice. However, my favorite is sporting clays. I like the different angles sporting clays provides. Most courses have stations with targets that simulate ducks floating into decoys, flying straight overhead, and passing at various angles.

When actually hunting ducks, three keys to being a good shot are to wait for shots that are well within range, to take your time when shooting (don't rush), and to try to kill only one duck at a time. When a flock comes in, many shooters aim into the mass and fire randomly instead of focusing on a single target. Such an effort usually results in embarrassing misses.

Many hunters concern themselves with holding the proper lead on ducks, and having the right lead is indeed necessary for clean kills. However, it's hard to *learn* leads. Each shot is different in terms of flight angle and speed. Some shots are head-on, some going away, some passing at 90 degrees. Some shots are at ducks floating in slowly or hovering over decoys, while others are at birds crossing at full speed. If you have to consciously think about how much lead to hold, you're probably going to miss.

Instead, let instinct take over. Concentrate on focusing on your target (look at a duck's eye) and simply following it with your shotgun. Your brain will automatically figure how much lead to hold, and if your gun fits properly and you have good shooting form you will connect. Yes, this sounds overly simple, but this instinctive method of achieving proper lead really works. Focus on the other shooting fundamentals, and lead will take care of itself.

As the seasons roll by and you gain experience at shooting ducks in a variety of situations, your skill will increase. If you practice enough, you'll learn to make long passing shots almost as easily as hovering-over-the-decoys shots. The truly good duck shot is the person who has confidence—gained through experience—and who swings and fires as mechanically as a great hitter swinging a baseball bat. In the duck blind, we might not all be Barry Bonds or Mark McGuires, but we can get enough hits to bag a limit and enjoy the satisfaction of a job well done.

Chapter Eight

Planning a Duck Hunting Trip

The miles clicked away in steady succession: tens, hundreds, then over two thousand as we drove ever north and west. We alternated 4-hour shifts at the wheel. We stopped only for gas and food and to exercise our two Labs, which endured the ride balled up on a quilt in the back of my hunting buddy's Blazer. As we traveled, day turned to night, then back to day. When darkness overtook us, the landscape was rolling and speckled with trees. When daylight returned, the scenery was flat and open.

Our route took us to St. Louis, then Kansas City, then north past Omaha, Sioux Falls, and Fargo. At Winnipeg we turned west again to Brandon, then back north past Dauphin and Swan River. Finally, after 37 hours on the road, we arrived at The Pas, Manitoba, looking to fulfill our duck hunting dreams.

This trip had been a long time in the making. My two partners and I had never hunted far from our homes in Tennessee, but we'd been fascinated by stories of vast waterfowl riches on

Duck hunters daydream about finding places where the birds are plentiful and competition is scarce.

Canada's prairie. We'd spent hours talking about going there. We'd read everything on the subject we could find. We'd called hunters and waterfowl biologists in both Manitoba and Saskatchewan. We'd pored over maps.

Finally we picked The Pas as our destination. It was the farthest north that grain was grown, and the rich Carrot River valley was pockmarked with marshes, which, according to our sources, were brimming with mallards and pintails. For us, it was the ultimate trip, as far as we could go, as exotic and promising as we could get. And now, finally, we were about to see if reality would live up to our high expectations.

It did, and then some! We spent the next five days in duck hunter's heaven. It was late September, and waterfowl were massing for their southbound migration. The grain harvest was late. Thousands of acres of barley and rye were swathed and laid out like a great banquet. Each morning unending flights of ducks would ascend from the marshes to gobble their fill, then return to their resting spots, where we'd be waiting.

There were no other hunters around. We could shoot wherever we wished. The ducks were oblivious of the dangers of decoys and calls and unmoving camouflaged forms hiding in the reeds. We could take our time, take turns, and bag our 8-bird limits in a grand, almost leisurely style.

The year was 1977, and that trip was the first of several we made to the North Country. We hunted The Pas a few straight years, then we branched into Saskatchewan, around Quill Lakes. In succeeding seasons we hunted the Dakotas and Nebraska. As a writer, I've also taken waterfowl trips into Arkansas, Mississippi, Louisiana, Texas, Missouri, Kansas, and Iowa. One especially memorable hunt for black ducks occurred in New Brunswick.

Part of the allure of duck hunting is trying new places. Duck hunters search for a special pot of gold. They daydream about finding spots where birds are plentiful and competition from other hunters is nil. Many relish the idea of "starting early," going somewhere where hunting season opens before their home season does, thus providing bonus time afield. Conversely, some hunters in northern states plan late-season trips into the South, after hunting in their home areas has shut down. Again, bonus hunting is the purpose.

Whichever, taking a road trip offers special pleasures for duck hunters. Great opportunities exist in all four flyways.

Hunters must simply commit to going, then set about researching their options and planning the details of their expedition.

Planning a Duck Hunting Road Trip

Good research and preparation are keys to a successful hunting trip. Finding the right spot, being there at the prime time, and
having the proper gear are all necessary for success. And sometimes even the best plans go awry when unforeseeable, uncon-
trollable circumstances arise. But that's why they call it "hunting" instead of "shooting." You can go to the best location on the
continent, but if the ducks have left, or if they don't fly, you'll
wind up staring at
empty skies.

Nevertheless,
planning a trip
involves stacking all
the odds in your
favor. You take care
of all the control-
lable factors, then
go on your trip and
hope for the best.

Hunters who visit pothole country can enjoy great waterfowl hunting before seasons back home come in.

Following is a list of considerations for planning a visit to
your duck hunting Shangri-La.

When to begin planning. The end of hunting season is the
best time to start planning a trip for the next season. The more
time you have to research and plan, the better. Also, some states

allocate non-resident licenses and permits through drawings, and application deadlines typically fall in early summer, so plan well in advance.

Where to go. This is the Grand Question. Picking the right spot is critical to a trip's success, and doing so requires plenty of research. Talk to other hunting acquaintances about trips they've taken. Check articles and advertisements in periodicals such as *Ducks Unlimited* magazine. Visit sport and travel shows and talk to outfitters. Contact references they provide, and quiz them thoroughly. Track down and interview biologists and game wardens in prospective hunting areas. Ask about number of birds, accessibility to good hunting, hunting pressure, etc. Collect information from state and provincial wildlife agencies and other public agencies that control public hunting lands. Many of these agencies have maps, hunting guides, sportsman's atlases, and other publications that are tremendously important in trip planning. Overall, be a detective and follow all leads to assemble information on prospective hunting spots.

Then make your choice. Commit to a spot based on what sounds most promising and appealing, then start focusing your efforts only on learning more about it.

One immediate consideration is choosing between booking with an outfitter or hunting on your own. A guided trip will obviously be more expensive, but it will leave less room for chance. (However, hiring a guide is *not* a guarantee of success.) On the other hand, if you take a self-guided trip, you may burn a couple of days learning your way around a new area and zeroing in on the action.

I've taken numerous guided and self-guided hunts, and both types were fun. Nothing against the guides, but I prefer to hunt on my own when feasible. I enjoy the challenge of putting a hunt together, and I gain great satisfaction when the pieces of the puzzle fall into place. Sure, I've had some failures (disasters?) on self-guided hunts, but when things have worked out, the pleasure has been far greater than if I'd been following someone else's direction.

When to go. This should be decided when researching the trip. Talk to the local biologist about when the duck population historically peaks in the area in question, and plan to go within a week of that time. Don't flirt with going earlier or later.

Once my partners and I decided to go to Saskatchewan two weeks later than we'd previously been there to try to intercept the "northern mallards." Just before our trip started, a major winter storm blew through the province. When we were driving north along the Missouri River between Kansas City and Omaha, we saw flight after flight of ducks and geese heading south. Despite being apprehensive, we kept going. When we got to Quill Lakes, we discovered that most waterfowl had already left Saskatchewan. That trip proved to be a bust because of bad timing.

What equipment to take. Being properly equipped is essential to a hunting trip's success. If you're going with an outfitter, this part is easy. He will tell you what to bring. But if you're hunting on your own, you must determine what equipment will be needed and how to get it there or arrange for it to be waiting when you arrive.

When my partners and I drive, we typically go in a four-wheel SUV and tow a boat with a portable blind. We load decoys and other large gear into the boat. Before departing, we pack the trailer's wheel bearings with fresh grease. We also check trailer tires for proper inflation, and we make sure the spare tire is inflated to the right pressure. (Make sure to include a lug wrench and jack that will work on the boat trailer.)

We carry our guns and duffels of smaller gear (boots, clothing, calls, shells, etc.) inside the truck. Our retriever now rides in a kennel in the rear of the vehicle.

© Bill Buckley

Head south and you can enjoy classic flooded timber hunting long after seasons up north have ended.

When packing, I refer to an equipment checklist that I've drawn up over the years. It lists everything a waterfowl hunter could possibly need on a trip. I certainly don't take everything on this inventory, but I have the option of considering whether or not I'll need each item. Using this list is good insurance against poor memory.

Using the Internet for Trip Planning

It is almost impossible to overstate the importance of using the Internet to research and plan a duck hunting trip. Hunters with good on-line skills can uncover a wealth of information about new hunting places. They can locate specific areas, review hunting regulations, apply for permits, purchase licenses, find phone numbers for biologists and game wardens, obtain travel directions, print out topo and aerial maps, chat with other hunters' who have been there, check the weather and perform other functions, all without leaving their computer terminals. In many cases, hunters can do everything over the "net" except figure out where to throw out the decoys.

Following is an overview of what's available on the Internet, including specific Web sites that can be useful in researching a duck hunting trip.

Federal/state/Canadian wildlife agency Web sites. Every federal, state and provincial wildlife agency in the U.S. and Canada maintains a Web site with detailed information about places to hunt, seasons, license requirements, permit procedures, etc. One easy way to access these Web sites is through www.fishandwildlife.org. Through this Web site, browsers have direct links to all U.S. and Canadian wildlife agency Web sites. Simply select a state or province and click with the mouse, and the Web site comes up.

Federal public hunting lands. The Web site www.Recreation.Gov is a partnership among federal land management agencies aimed at providing a single, easy-to-use source for information about recreation—including hunting—on federal lands. This site allows browsers to search for areas by state, by recreational activity, or by agency. Each hunting spot is described (including directions to get there), and a phone number is provided for follow-up information.

Federal agency Web sites. Hunters wanting additional information about access to federal lands should check out each managing agency's Web site. These sites include: U.S. Fish and Wildlife Service, www.fws.gov; USDA Forest Service, www.fs.fed.us; U.S. Bureau of Land Management, www.blm.gov; U.S. Army Corps of Engineers, www.usace.army.mil; National Park Service, www.nps.gov; U.S. Bureau of Reclamation, www.usbr.gov; and the Tennessee Valley Authority, www.tva.gov. Through these sites, web browsers can navigate to regional or sub-regional offices to locate public lands. They can also obtain names and phone numbers of land managers and wildlife biologists who can offer first-person advice on where good duck hunting exists. (Hint: If you have trouble finding information about hunting opportunities on a particular Web site, try clicking "Search" on the main menu, then type in the keyword "hunting" or "recreation" to focus your quest.)

Private Web sites. There are literally thousands of Web sites on the Internet for hunters, and many offer specific information on public hunting areas, guide services, etc. The best way to find these sites is to call up a good search engine (www.yahoo.com, www.AltaVista.com, www.google.com), type in specific keywords (i.e., "waterfowl hunting"), then browse through related links and click on those that look interesting. (Check out Ducks Unlimited's official Web site, www.ducks.org.)

Also, many of these Web sites feature message boards that allow web browsers to contact other hunters and seek information about specific areas. Hunters frequently become buddies through back-and-forth conversations, like members of a "virtual hunting club," sometimes even sharing hunts with each other. However, it's always a good idea to verify recommendations given by individuals with a wildlife management professional familiar with the area.

Ten Great Duck Hunting Destinations

Good duck hunting can be found throughout the U.S., Canada, and northern Mexico, but some areas stand out above the rest. They do so because of their large concentrations of birds and opportunities for hunters to enjoy them. Following is a list of ten great duck hunting destinations and initial contact information for hunters who would like to learn more about them.

Central Flyway Reservoirs. One very good, little-used duck hunting opportunity exists on several reservoirs in Kansas and Oklahoma. When cold weather freezes shallow water in these states, large concentrations of dabbling ducks collect on these reservoirs, which are mostly open to public hunting. In Kansas, good prospects are Kirwin, Glen Elder, Milford, John Redmond, Marion, and Norton Lakes. Contact: Kansas Department of Wildlife & Parks, 620-672-5911; www.kdwp.state.ks.us. (This Web site features waterfowl counts that are updated weekly.) In Oklahoma, good duck lakes include Eufaula, Oologah, Kaw, Grand Lake of the Cherokees,

Texoma, Hulah, Copan, and Gibson. Contact: Oklahoma Department of Wildlife Conservation, 405-521-3851; www.wildlifedepartment.com. Also, hunting is better on all these reservoirs when water levels are higher than normal. Before coming to hunt here, check water levels on these reservoirs on Army Corp of Engineers/BLM Web sites.

Eastern Arkansas. The table-flat country around Stuttgart, Arkansas, is known as the "Rice and Duck Capital of the World." This region is the primary wintering ground for mallards in the Mississippi Flyway. Its rice fields and flooded timber bottoms attract a million or more of these and other ducks in a good season. An extensive network of guides and lodges caters to visiting hunters. Freelancers can find good hunting on several state wildlife management areas and national wildlife refuges (especially the White River and Cache River refuges), depending on water conditions. Expect heavy hunting pressure on more popular areas when duck numbers are high. When rainfall is abundant, best hunting occurs in flooded bottomland hardwoods and fields bordering these rivers. But when conditions are dry, fields and reservoirs pumped with water hold the most birds. Contact: Arkansas Game & Fish Commission; 501-223-6300; www.agfc.state.ar.us; also, contact Stuttgart, Arkansas Chamber of Commerce; 870-673-1602; www.stuttgartarkansas.com.

East-Central Florida. Florida? Ducks? This state is known more for snow birds than waterfowl, but don't be deceived. Florida boasts the highest success rate on ducks (birds per hunter per day) of all states in the Atlantic Flyway. In the right areas, pintails, wigeon, gadwall, and teal are abundant, and Florida mottled ducks are also available. The best spots are the Merritt Island National Wildlife Refuge near Titusville and the upper St. Johns River basin, which extends from Indian River County north to Orange County. Merritt Island has the largest concentration of birds, but hunting is rigidly controlled through permit allocation. Hunting in the St. Johns basin is wide open. Hundreds of square miles of lakes and marshes are available, and hunters must scout by boat to find where ducks are concentrated. (Puzzle and Winder Lakes are perennial hotspots.) Contact: Florida Fish & Wildlife Conservation Commission, 850-488-1960; www.floridaconservation.org.

Mississippi Delta Country. The delta country of northwest Mississippi can be duck paradise. This region—a mix of agricultural fields and swampy hardwood bottoms—contains several national wildlife refuges that attract vast numbers of mallards and other dabbling ducks each winter. Opportunities abound for hunting on both private and public land. When the weather is cold up north and water conditions are good, the Mississippi Delta can offer some of the best duck hunting anywhere in green timber, sloughs, and flooded fields. The Mississippi Outfitter's Guide lists commercial guides and lodges in this state. Contact: Mississippi Division of Tourism; 800-927-6378; www.visitmississippi.org; Mississippi Department of Wildlife, Fisheries & Parks; 601-432-2400; www.mdfwp.com.

Planning a Duck Hunting Trip

Moses Lake/South Columbia River Basin, Washington.
Two regions in Washington State offer superlative mallard hunting in uncrowded settings. The Bureau of Reclamation owns 300,000 acres in the Moses Lake area that is managed by the Washington Department of Fish & Wildlife. This large holding includes numerous potholes accessible to boat-in and hike-in hunters. Also, good hunting can be had off the sand islands in nearby Potholes Reservoir. On a good year, more than a half-million mallards concentrate here during peak of migration. But when the potholes freeze over, these ducks shift down to the South Columbia Basin at the confluence of the Columbia and Snake Rivers (Tri-Cities area—Richland, Kennewick and Pasco). Here, freelance opportunity is available on national wildlife refuges and on Army Corp of Engineers land along the Snake. Guide service is available in both areas. Contact: Washington Department of Fish & Wildlife, 360-902-2515; www.wa.gov/wdfw. Also, many guide services are advertised in the Migratory Waterfowl & Upland Game Season pamphlet available from the Washington Department of Fish & Wildlife.

North American Prairie Pothole Region. This immense area is almost too large to describe. It spans parts of the Canadian provinces of Manitoba, Saskatchewan, and Alberta and the U.S. states of North and South Dakota. This is the region where the majority of the continent's dabbling ducks are produced. Then, as summer changes to fall, adult and juvenile birds gather in large pre-migration flocks, typically feeding in grainfields and marshes and loafing on ponds, lakes, reservoirs, and rivers.

Chapter Eight

Hunting seasons in these provinces and states usually open before the ducks migrate. Hunters who venture here can enjoy this great waterfowl abundance before seasons back home come in. Hunts can be conducted either in dry feeding fields or over water. Hunting opportunities are as varied as the region is vast. Every dedicated duck hunter owes himself at least one road trip into pothole country sometime in his life. Trip-planning information is available through a variety of sources, namely provincial and state wildlife agencies, conservation/hunter organizations such as Ducks Unlimited, guide services, and others.

Reelfoot Lake, Tennessee. This 7,000-acre cypress-and-sawgrass lake in northwest Tennessee (near Tiptonville) is a major wintering area for Mississippi Flyway ducks, especially mallards. These birds concentrate on nearby federal and state refuges, and terrific shooting is available on the lake proper and in surrounding flooded fields. Most hunting here is done from fixed blinds with guides. Reelfoot guides are noted as being some of the most skilled duck callers in the country. The beauty and lore of Reelfoot add to the attraction of a trip here. Contact: Blue Bank Resort; 731-253-6878; www.bluebankresort.com; Tennessee Wildlife Resources Agency; 731-423-5725; www.state.tn.us/twra.

Sandhills Region, Nebraska. The Nebraska Sandhills span some 19,000 square miles in the north-central part of this state (between Alliance and Bassett). Tucked away between the rolling sandhills are hundreds of natural lakes and wetlands that hatch an abundance of dabbling ducks, and that attract hundreds of thousands more when the fall migration pushes in birds from farther north. These small waters are mostly on private ranches, but many are accessible to hunters who ask permission. Plan to hunt before freezeup, which normally occurs by mid-November. Contact: Nebraska Game & Parks Commission, 402-471-0641; www.outdoornebraska.org.

South Louisiana Marsh Country. The coastal region of south Louisiana (south of Interstate 10) is the terminus point for the Mississippi flyway, and it is an area of enormous waterfowl wealth and hunting heritage. From Cameron Parish in the west to Plaquemines in the east, the Gulf coastal marsh and bordering rice fields are magnets to a broad variety of dabbling and diving ducks. On a good year more than 4 million ducks will be counted here when the Louisiana Department of Wildlife & Fisheries conducts its late-winter waterfowl count. Hunting these birds is a way of life in the predominant Cajun culture, and there's plenty opportunity for outsiders to tag along. Guide services are numerous; guides can be contacted through Chambers of Commerce in Lake Charles, Lafayette, Morgan City, Houma, Venice, and other coastal towns. Also, several refuges and wildlife management areas have public hunting areas where visitors can strike out on their own. (Take a GPS so you won't get lost.) Great food, times and duck hunting are hallmarks of this land of *joie de vivre*! Contact: Louisiana Department of Wildlife & Fisheries, 225-765-2346; www.wlf.state.la.us.

Texas Playa Region. The Texas Panhandle north of Amarillo is dotted with thousands of shallow playa basins that hold water during wet years. Some playas exceed 200 acres in size, but most span less than 10 acres. Together, these lakes make up one of the most important waterfowl areas in North America. Each fall several million ducks and geese migrate through this region. When water conditions are good, many mallards, pintails, teal, gadwall, and other ducks linger here for extended periods. But despite this abundance of birds, hunting pressure on the playas is relatively light. One waterfowl biologist calls this "the undiscovered part of Texas." Hunters can book with one of the area's guide services (check with the Chambers of Commerce in Amarillo and Dumas), or they can drive to this region and hunt on their own. Most landowners will grant access for free or for a small daily trespass fee. Contact: Texas Parks & Wildlife Office in Canyon: 806-655-3782; www.tpwd.state.tx.us. Before coming here, call this office to inquire about which area of the Panhandle has best water conditions in the playas.